How to Get Along with Your Church

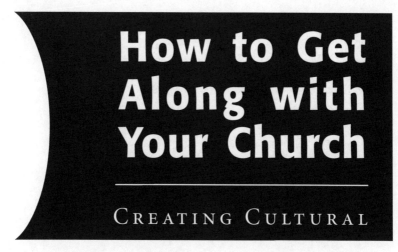

How to Get Along with Your Church

CREATING CULTURAL

CAPITAL FOR DOING MINISTRY

George B. Thompson Jr.

Foreword by David L. Wallace Sr.

The Pilgrim Press
Cleveland

To Rev. Dr. Kenneth B. Smith Sr.

President, The Chicago Theological Seminary, 1985–1998

pastor, civic leader, friend of students, mentor

The Pilgrim Press, 700 Prospect Avenue, Cleveland, Ohio 44115-1100

© 2001 George B. Thompson Jr.

All rights reserved. Published 2001

Printed in the United States of America on acid-free paper

06 05 04 03 02 01   5 4 3 2 1

Library of Congress Cataloging-in-Publication Data

Thompson, George B. (George Button), 1951–

    How to get along with your church : creating cultural capital for doing ministry /

    George B. Thompson, Jr. ; foreword by David L. Wallace, Sr.

        p.   cm.

    Includes bibliographical references.

    ISBN 0-8298-1437-x (alk. paper)

    1. Pastoral theology.   I. Title.

BV4011.3 .T46   2001

253—dc21

2001036796

Contents

Foreword by David L. Wallace Sr. • vii

Preface • xi

1. **Land Mines:** How Well Do You Know What You're Getting Into? • 1

2. **"Welcome to the Family!"** Have You Been Adopted Yet ? • 27

3. **Making It Count:** How Does "Busyness" Turn into Ministry? • 45

4. **Effective Delivery:** Who Can Carry Bad News? • 61

5. **Ahead of the Troops:** How Do Pastors Become Leaders? • 73

6. **Handling Conflict:** What If Things Go Sour? • 87

7. **Saying Goodbye:** When Is It Time to Move On? • 113

   Appendix: For Denominational Officials • 137

   Notes • 145

Foreword

WHEN I SERVED in the parish, I think I could have avoided some serious land mines if I had been exposed to the insights of this book. One such incident looms large in my memory. As a young, new, and eager pastor, I thought that church polity was supposed to govern the church's every action. I had heard so many folk talk about our Presbyterian form of government in such glowing and majestic terms, it seemed to be some kind of golden rulebook. Consequently, when I reviewed the *Book of Order* and someone in my new congregation noted that it never had conducted an audit of its finances, I was the first to declare that the constitution must be obeyed! To use a colloquialism, I rammed the *Book of Order* down their throats.

Immediately, the storm clouds began to form. The current finance committee mistakenly drew the conclusion that an investigation was being undertaken to uncover some impropriety in their work. Even though this had nothing to do with my zeal, it was difficult to dispel their perception. As we discovered in due time, the church's finances were in good condition. In fact, this church had more money than it ever had before. This was due partly to the finance committee's good stewardship and attention to every penny of the church's funds. Yet at the conclusion of the audit, despite my praise of their work, the entire committee resigned en masse. I thought to myself, "Oh, what a mess I have made of a very simple situation!"

Understanding a church's culture offers a fresh new lens for providing deeper insight into why churches like mine behave the way they do. This is the most significant contribution provided by George Thompson's book,

How to Get Along with Your Church. Earlier writers have drawn on the so-
cial sciences to address the realities of congregations, as I discovered in my
Doctor of Ministry program at McCormick Theological Seminary. There,
I was exposed to teachers who were preaching the gospel of organizational
transformation for churches based on learnings from the social sciences.
Prominent on the reading list in those days was James MacGregor Burns,
Leadership; Robert Worley, *Dry Bones Breathe!;* and John Adams, *Trans-
forming Work.*

In this groundbreaking volume, Thompson cuts right to the chase and
focuses on the importance of pastors becoming students of culture. He
argues that a grasp of the complexities of culture help a pastor to understand more skillfully the behavior patterns and relationships in the life of
the church. The book is clear and engaging to read. It is brought to life by
the author's adept ability to use anecdotal experiences in explaining the
subject and suggesting conceptual tools for dealing with common pastoral
problems.

A clearer understanding of my old parish's culture and how it operates
would have placed in my hands some significant insights for handling the
situation. I would have known from the beginning that someone with a
little more cultural capital and time invested in the community would have
been more effective at bringing the news of our polity's requirement concerning audits. Then, perhaps after a period of education and long prayer-
ful discussion, the ruling board and I could have implemented a change
process for a first-time audit with minimal conflict.

In those early days of my ministry, I could have been informed by some
of the invaluable points that Professor Thompson makes in this book. From
today's vantage point years later, it is liberating for me to realize that new
pastors should not be in a hurry to tell congregations what is wrong and
what they must do to improve. Consequently, in my role as the dean of a
seminary, I share with my students that new pastors should take on a posture of learning, not rushing to make fundamental changes in their new
parishes.

The utility of this book, however, is not simply in its suggested practical
techniques. I also am impressed that Thompson does not approach his

topic monolithically. Rather, I believe that his model of cultural capital can be applied to diverse racial groups. This feature is especially important today: Theological education seeks to respond to the church's own pluralism, providing relevant teaching experiences for growing racial and/or ethnic representations.

How to Get Along with Your Church makes us fully aware that one size will not fit all situations. In other words, the writer challenges his readers to become students of their particular cultures, which may be African American, Asian American, European American, Hispanic American, or American Indian. It does not matter what one's culture may be. Leaders who know and understand the insights provided by this book will be empowered to be more effective leaders of the church.

For those who are involved with theological education, this book helps give a better appreciation for what the Greeks called *paideia* (i.e. "instructions" or "learnings"). Thompson's cultural framing of challenges to the pastoral role will be useful in enriching and enhancing course offerings in theological institutions, especially in the area of church administration. With the tools that the book provides, seminarians will be better prepared for parish leadership. As a book for the church, it has an even wider appeal. Lay leaders and denominational executives who deal with conflict, the pervasive problem of "blaming" and "faultfinding" in the church, can use it as well. I would strongly recommend its being utilized by lay leaders in a retreat setting or officer training event. This cultural model provides leaders with some wonderful insights and knowledge to help lift them into their better selves, so that an environment is created in which church folk can work together.

I learned some important things about ministry here, because *How to Get Along with Your Church* provides cutting-edge material. It places in our hands tools, insights, and freshly presented information on how leadership in the church should operate. It will aid us as we continue our journey of faith on "the Old Ship of Zion," facing the rough seas of conflict and chaos and the torrential winds of challenge and change. If we take what Thompson has to say here seriously, perhaps, like the apostle Paul, we will be able to develop a deeper and richer faith in God. It will be a faith that inspires us to do like Paul, to put on the whole armor of God, embracing both the spiritual and temporal wisdom that comes from being students of culture. It will be a faith that inspires us to embrace knowledge, insights, and yes, even anchors to help us withstand on the evil day and, having done everything, to stand firm.

DAVID L. WALLACE SR., DEAN
Johnson C. Smith Theological Seminary
The Interdenominational Theological Center
Atlanta, Georgia

Preface

TWO DECADES AGO, my denomination used to bring together young pastors not too long after they had begun their first ministries. These conferences were held regionally around the country, in a retreat setting, to give newly ordained neophytes in the parish a chance to rest, recreate, and reflect on their first years. Research had indicated that the highest rate of pastoral "dropouts" occurred between the third and fifth years out of seminary. The "young pastors' seminars" brought the same group of pastors together, three years in a row, to support and encourage their formative years of vocation.

Part of the agenda in each seminar was listening to each pastor talk about how things had been going. Although the series of seminars begin typically in the pastors' third year out, some of us—like myself—already were in our second positions. I remember much of that first seminar so vividly, in part because I was hurting so much. I had left my first position as assistant pastor after eighteen months, struggling not to feel like a failure. Now here I was, pastor of a small church in a very small town, already feeling frustrated, confused, and lonely.

I was not alone in those feelings. A few of the other pastors at the seminar that I attended were unhappy as well. That much was obvious from the stories we told, even though the details varied. On the other hand, many of the other young pastors in our seminar seemed satisfied, confident, and energetic. They appeared to be having little or no trouble in their churches; some of them were practically ebullient when describing their work. What made the difference? Was there something innately wrong with those of us young pastors who were struggling? Were we incompetent, while our colleagues more capable? Or did we choose "bad" churches, while our new friends managed to luck into a "good" church?

In some important ways, this book is an attempt to make sense out of such questions that for me have been so personal. It is based on the conviction that it is possible for pastors to become adept at learning "what they are walking into" as they enter a new congregation. This conviction applies whether that pastor has been called by the congregation or appointed by a bishop. Hence, it is written for the tens of thousands of pastors who, in responding to God's call on their lives, willingly have put themselves in the position of moving from church to church throughout their years of pastoral service.

As pastors proceed through their ministry, they pick up insights and advice from others whose advanced location on the ministerial journey makes them more seasoned. Of course, I have received such "wisdom," too; over the years, I have found myself holding on to some of it while questioning and abandoning others of it. "It isn't all true, or at least not always true," I concluded. So don't expect this book to offer you a plethora of pithy, quotable sayings.

What makes the present work different from a collection of oral nuggets is its intentional foundation. My pastoral journey since those young pastors' seminars includes more study and reflection on ministry itself. I have come to believe that cultural anthropology—among other disciplines in the social sciences—can be utilized as a potent ally in pastoral ministry. This branch of anthropology looks at the overall life of a community, seeking to discern patterns of behavior and meaning that are shared among its members. As a research discipline, anthropology is identified most frequently with Third World countries and "primitive" settings; however, there is nothing inherent in the nature of this discipline that confines it to the study of people who appear to be "different" from us. This limitation of anthropological subjects says more about Western intellectual bias than it does about the usefulness of anthropology to illuminate virtually any human community.

In other words, it is high time that we begin discovering what a resource like anthropology can reveal about our common institutions, including churches.[1] Congregations themselves create communities, and those communities in turn create, nurture, and transmit culture.[2] Because of this basic fact, culture itself is very complex, nuanced, and sometimes seemingly inscrutable. A pastor who arrives at her new appointment after annual conference might assume that she knows enough about the congregation because it is "similar" to the church that she just left. That assumption might be the case—or it might not! Her ability to do effective ministry within that congregation will be directly affected by that one, perhaps dangerous, assumption.

In this book, then, we are going to explore the important task of getting along with one's church. By this, I do not mean to imply that the focus of every pastor's ministry should be merely to make every single church member happy all the time, or simply to capitulate to the congregation's every wish and whim. Besides being impossible to fulfill, such a strategy would not allow the pastor to understand genuinely the congregation's life and folkways. Neither would it prepare the congregation to face the world of change that is pursuing all religious bodies in the twenty-first century. If for no other reason, a pastor who gets inside the church's culture is in a much better position to help that church learn to adapt. Effective ministry in the future is all about learning, both by the pastor and by the congregation.

In their book on doing administration in the African American Baptist church, Floyd Massey Jr. and Samuel Berry McKinney tell the story of a young, frustrated pastor who sought out the advice of a seasoned minister. The neophyte was not getting along with his congregation. The elder, wiser pastor listened to the young one's story as they sat on the former's front porch, while nearby freight trains moved in and out of the switching station. Pointing out the source of the distracting sounds, the elder asked the junior to observe what the trains were doing. He complied, and his elder used the young man's comments as the basis for the valued advice. Massey and McKinney conclude the story by summarizing: "Every pastor must be willing to back up, hook up, and then move out from where they are to where they must go."[3]

Back up, hook up, and then move out. . . . Here is the key to getting along with your church. But how does a pastor do it? It is done by developing "cultural capital" within the congregation. "Cultural capital" is a term that has been used in various academic circles.[4] In part, this phrase is used to describe the way that people gain the ability to participate significantly in a community, by becoming accepted and honoring its values. For organizations, this ability derives from a person "paying their dues." We are familiar with this notion when we say such things as, "I invested so much of my time and energy into that project; I just had to see it turn out well." Human beings tend to assume that there is a relationship between what someone "puts into" something and what they "get out" of it. The specifically cultural spin on capital comes into play as we begin to recognize the various ways in which groups expect their members to behave and express meaning.

In this regard, churches are no different from any other organization. In some ways, cultural capital might be even more important in congregations because of the basic, theological purposes for which they exist. Congregations want pastors who appreciate what they themselves have invested in their life, how they seek to live out the gospel in their distinctive ways. As we will see, no amount of information on a church bulletin or profile can tell that rich story.

Anthony Gittins, in his wonderful and readable book about cross-cultural mission, *Gifts and Strangers*, discusses how mission work involves the complex phenomenon of "inculturation."[5] Inculturation for Gittins refers to the interwoven experiences that take place when one people convey the message of Jesus and the Gospel to another people. As I read what Gittins has to say about this process of sharing, I am struck by how it sounds so much like what a new pastor faces with a congregation. I quote two passages, to illustrate:

> In the first place, we must never forget that we go to real people in real situations amid real problems but that these people have real wisdom and real aspirations; to overlook these truths would lead to our patronizing others and ultimately treating them as no better than objects. Secondly, we cannot believe that the people to whom we go have been forgotten or abandoned by God. It is therefore a serious obligation of ours to discern the presence of God in their lives; and this in turn demands that we ourselves be led by the Spirit of God. . . .

Mission is delicate in its challenge and complex in its execution . . . we are inevitably drawn into new relationships, and other lives, and other histories and other aspirations; and the agenda which we bring must at some point encounter the life-experience and social context of those people into whose lives we erupt.[6]

If we substituted the term "pastoral ministry" for the word "mission" above, we would be reading in the text from Gittins a most apt description of a pastor's tasks and challenges. What follows in this book elaborates on Gittins's claims, in the same spirit and with a similar anthropological outlook. Readers familiar with my earlier book, *Futuring Your Church: Finding Your Vision and Making It Work*, will recognize some of the same concepts and similar applications.

This book is written primarily with pastors in mind, most of whom will end up spending some of their years in solo situations. This does not mean, however, that pastors at churches with other staff and clergy will not find the ideas here to be useful. Rather, staff pastors, directors of Christian education, music ministers, and others might discover that the complexity within their congregations makes a lot more sense, once they have discovered who has which cultural capital! For instance, why do many multiple-pastor churches have a hard time treating all of their ordained staff people as ministers in their own right? Answering this question for their own situation would help many assistant and associate pastors. If they are trying to promote themselves, cultural capital might be harder to accrue than they imagine. If they are trying to do authentic ministry in that particular congregation, they can benefit the church, as well as learn some valuable insights along the way.

This book also will be useful for judicatory officials who are directly involved in relationships between pastors and congregations (bishops, district superintendents, presiding elders, executive presbyters, regional and conference ministers, etc.). The appendix suggests to such officials the kinds of questions to ask and the tactics to utilize as they participate in matches between pastors and churches. Many of these women and men already use the insights found in this book in an intuitive way. The book will give them a clear language and framework that should enhance their discussions and decision-making about placement.

I have one other, much broader, goal for this book. It is to help restore some balance in Western and American assumptions about the nature of persons and group existence. This "self-society" discussion has taken place much more in the academic arena than in popular, or even ecclesial, circles.[7] The modern world gradually developed a notion of human existence that has lifted the individual person to such a degree that relationships with community are difficult to recognize, appreciate, or engage. Ironically, however, the church itself promulgates biblical metaphors (e.g., "the body of Christ" as in 1 Cor. 12) that suggest an understanding between individuals and groups that is more mutual. An anthropological framework, such as the one utilized here, helps to anchor these normative theological claims in descriptive, measurable categories. In practical terms, this means that pastors can benefit tremendously by applying notions such as "cultural capital" to their analysis of congregations. It is a notion that implicitly begins to correct our modern (and post-modern) skew toward individualism.

In some ways, as I have already intimated, this discussion is intensely personal. If I had understood as a new pastor even some of what is presented in the following chapters, both the congregations and I could have benefited. For myself, I would have been more relaxed as I commenced my ministry, less concerned to "produce," and more tuned-in to the congregation's subtleties. I would have accepted a "learning mode" on my part as necessary and instructive. This would have helped me respond more openly and willingly to the church rather than supposing that I had to initiate or impose things on it. Simply put, I was not adequately equipped to know what I was getting into as a new pastor. Conceptual tools like the ones in this book fill that void for me; I think that they can do the same for many others, too.

I have conceived the basic challenges to a pastor's cultural capital in terms of the span between arriving and leaving a pastorate. From the time that the pastor knows that he or she will serve this one church, to the time that he or she departs from it, what does cultural capital help us understand about that pastor's ability to do ministry? The following chapters will address several questions that are likely to appear, in one way or another, throughout a pastor's tenure.

Since local churches consist of groups of human beings, insights from the social sciences help to make sense out of what occurs in those groups. Pastors must realize that their ability to do effective ministry depends on their acquisition of cultural capital within that particular congregation. It is to the appropriation of such capital—and the authentic Christian ministry that can result—that this book is dedicated.

It is a most pleasant opportunity to teach for the Interdenominational Theological Center. Its students represent an array of denominational traditions almost as diverse as Christianity itself. These students bring to class their faith, their church experience, and their willingness to be more fully equipped as servants of God. Through their honest sharing and probing questions, the idea for this book was born.

I thank Rev. Ms. Ruth Hicks, associate executive for ministry, Presbytery of Greater Atlanta, and Rev. Mr. Robby Carroll, director of the Atlanta Center for Counseling and Development, for encouraging me to write and for reading the manuscript. I also thank my brother, Chaplain (Major) Robert W. Thompson, U.S. Army, and his wife Pamala for giving the manuscript a "real readers" test. Finally, I would like to thank my new colleague and friend, Rev. Dr. David L. Wallace Sr., dean of Johnson C. Smith Theological Seminary of the Interdenominational Theological Center, who graciously agreed to write the foreword.

Land Mines

How Well Do You Know What You're Getting Into?

"I THOUGHT I KNEW ... "

MARY JOHNSON WAS A conscientious pastor. After years of teaching school, she finally had responded to the call to pastoral ministry. She completed her seminary training and was ordained at the mature age of 53. It was a happy day for her and her family! Mary was pleased to accept a call as an associate pastor of a large, suburban congregation. Before too long, however, the strain of some tense staff relationships led her to "try her wings" as a solo pastor. She accepted a call to serve a small church in a nearby city.

During the interview process, Mary and the search committee had talked about the most obvious difference between them: She was of European descent, and the congregation was Chinese. Native pastors were hard to attract to their city, and Mary was eager to prove herself a good pastor. The search committee concluded that she would be a satisfactory choice.

For the first few months, Mary sought to get to know the congregation, and she felt as though things were going well. Within two more years, however, she had resigned as pastor, feeling discouraged, bewildered, tired, and even somewhat angry. What had happened?

Mary thought that she had tried to be sensitive to cultural issues as she began her pastorate with the Chinese congregation. She knew that there would be differences, compared with her prior experience in European American, white-collar churches. What she realized—only too late—was that the Chinese custom of extending polite public behavior toward her as pastor did not necessarily equate to full approval of her behavior. Whenever an issue in the church had come up, Mary had spoken her mind. She was direct about her opinions, even though she tried hard to do so respectfully. That forthrightness did not sit well with the mostly older membership who still highly valued traditional social customs. Board members began to appear evasive to Mary, hard to understand, even duplicitous at times. She was not picking up on their tacit signals about her style. Eventually the dynamics became so enigmatic to Mary that she decided it was time to go.

CULTURES CROSSING

It is tempting to suppose that Mary's unhappy pastoral experience is due simply to differences in national cultures. Common American assumptions about the role of women and leadership style do indeed vary from those in Asian societies. In retrospect, we could tell Mary that perhaps it was inevitable that she and the Chinese congregation would end up at odds with each other. Yet, even if our assessment were not that harsh, framing the analysis solely in terms of nationality undermines an opportunity for greater insight. Mary's "failure" illustrates a similar kind of potential "failure" that faces any pastor who serves even in her or his own ethnic group.

In other words, the danger in any new pastorate is that the pastor will not relate strongly enough to the culture of that particular church community. When this fails to take place, the pastor has a difficult time being effective. Since effective ministry is the goal of this book, the first question we have to ask of the pastor entering a new parish is, "How well do you know what you are getting into?"

This book is based on the premise that "culture" provides rich resources to pastors for understanding their churches. Furthermore, pastors who lead their congregations in authentic, effective gospel ministry do so as they are perceived as having invested themselves in that congregation. This notion of investing in a church's culture is what we will refer to in this book as "cultural capital." In her two-and-a-half years as pastor of the Chinese congregation, Mary was not able to develop sufficient cultural capital. Part of the reason for this lack was her ignorance, in spite of their conversations and her earnest efforts.

How many times have you heard a pastoral colleague say, "If I only had known then what I know now, I would have done things differently in that church!" I have heard it said, and I have said it myself. This opening chapter sets the stage for helping a pastor to develop cultural capital, by tackling what could be the first question every pastor who is new to a church needs to ask: "How well do I know what I am getting into?"

PAUL, THE CULTURAL CAPITALIST

The need to develop cultural capital is recognized—if implicitly—even by such an ancient authority as the apostle Paul. In 1 Corinthians, the itinerant, tent-making pastor is writing to a congregation who seems to have gotten mixed up about some basic elements of the young Christian faith. Not unrelatedly, the Corinthian church also does not have much regard for Paul's leadership. Paul spends more time than he probably would have preferred in defending his right to preach and teach in the name of Christ.

In chapter 9 of 1 Corinthians, Paul's rhetorical self-defense takes an interesting turn. He speaks of his freedom and rights, but even more of his active self-denial. Paul claims that he adapts himself to whatever religious or ethnic group with whom he is associating: "To the Jews I became as a Jew (v. 20a); To those outside the law I became as one outside the law (v. 21a); To the weak I became weak (v. 22a)." Whether Jew or Gentile or ostracized, no social group of Paul's day was beyond his reach. He had a clear goal in mind: "I have become all things to all people, that I might by all means save some" (v. 22b).

In the language of this book, Paul worked at developing cultural capital so that all kinds of people would respond to the gospel. He was most willing to cross the kinds of contemporary cultural settings that many other Jews would have eschewed. Somehow, though, Paul "earned the right to be heard" outside of his own strict religious network. All we have to do today to realize what a task Paul faced is to think about trying to do the same thing. Most of us would rather stay with what to us is culturally comfortable. In his zeal for the gospel, Paul learned what he had to learn about his new audiences. Now there is a lesson for anyone who aspires to be a pastor!

OUTLINING THE PROCESS

In order to set the stage for our exploration of cultural capital, this first chapter will introduce a number of related concepts. Some of them will reappear in later chapters. For our present purpose, we want to lay the foundation of a cultural lens that can be used for looking at congregations. This will make it possible to discuss, in this chapter, ways that pastors can become more adept at learning what makes their church tick. Be prepared: You may be surprised!

Not all pastors begin pastoral tenure through the same process. Some denominations operate by the congregational call process, others by some form of appointment by a denominational official (i.e., a bishop). We will discuss the implications of this cultural model of churches for both ways of beginning: for the pastor who has a say in deciding on a call, and for the pastor who receives an appointment. Let us begin this examination by referring to a document often used in call processes: the church profile.

WHAT YOU SEE IS NOT WHAT YOU GET!

In several denominations, it is expected or required that a congregation seeking a pastor first prepare a document for potential candidates to read. That document, sometimes known as the "church profile" or "church information form," contains a variety of information. It is the congregation's version of a résumé or dossier. Prepared by the pastor search committee, the profile typically includes a set of basic statistics about the congregation, such as:

- year founded
- current membership (compared to a few years earlier)
- ratios in membership for gender, race/ethnicity, age, education, occupations, income levels
- current year's operating budget
- summary of programs and levels of participation
- staffing configuration, full- and part-time
- summary of physical facilities and debt

Statistics in a profile also often cover the neighborhood or town in which the church's facilities are located. They usually cover similar topics, such as:

- population of area
- age and racial/ethnic ratios
- education and income levels
- occupations and businesses/industries
- recreational, cultural, educational resources

The information about the church has to be gathered from congregational records, and some will have been brought together just for this purpose. Data from the community is usually available through municipal agencies or the area chamber of commerce.

In addition to these kinds of statistics, church profiles often include some narrative sections. In these, the search committee tells something about its church's self-understanding, sense of mission, recent major events, congregational issues, and expectations for the near future. A separate section will summarize what the church expects of its next pastor. Information pertaining to the next pastor's compensation package, vacation, and continuing education terms also is often included.

Anyone who has served on a search committee can tell you how much time and energy is required to gather and arrange the statistical and narrative information outlined above. It is a lot of work! Yet, in spite of a judicious effort on the church profile, the search committee still might end up not asking itself two key questions:

1. What have we learned about our congregation?
2. What will this profile tell pastor candidates about us?

These key questions might not get the crucial attention they deserve because the deeper dimensions of a congregation's life and character are not tangible. These deeper dimensions by nature are cultural. In order to appreciate how complex and subtle culture can be, let us introduce a few terms here. The concepts that these terms represent open the door to insights about the relationships between all the profile data and the fascinating world of the church that lives within those data. While statistics give us "cool" information, culture is the "warm" stuff, just as real, and definitely more elusive.

INITIAL CONCEPTS OF CULTURE

In this section, we will define and explain several concepts. These are foundational concepts for the framework of cultural capital. They will appear throughout other chapters of the book as they are applied to various themes.

CULTURE

Simply stated, "culture" is "shared meaning and behavior." This brief phrase suggests several things: that culture is something that people have in association with others; that culture stands for things that are important to people, things that they value; and that culture is acted out in the things that people do. When Americans recite the Pledge of Allegiance or watch fireworks on Independence Day, they are sharing meaning and behavior; they are expressing elements of culture.

LEVELS OF CULTURE

Yet, as I already have suggested, culture—though very much a part of human experience—is not necessarily easy to interpret. That is because it exists at three distinct levels.[1] Being able to distinguish the three levels is a crucial first step in learning what is going on in any particular culture, including that of a church.

Whenever we visit somewhere new to us, we immediately notice the ways in which the people there make things and do things that are different. Structures for living and working, objects for daily use, rituals and activities, dress, ways in which persons interact—these and other kinds of items are visible and easily noticeable. Taken all together, they are the culture's *artifacts*. As such, they are easy to observe. What gets us into trouble, however, is when we think we know what those unfamiliar artifacts mean.

Consider, for example, the Methodist minister who attends Annual Conference and receives a new appointment. Let's say that Rev. Lovejoy already has served two churches, both with about two hundred members each, mostly older and middle-aged members, in small towns that are county seats. Her new appointment is to a church that also has about two hundred members, except that it is located in the largest city in the conference. Also, the new parish is in a neighborhood of that city that is rapidly changing its ethnic makeup. Rev. Lovejoy arrives at the new church building and observes that it looks very much like the buildings of her previous two charges. She might be inclined to think to herself, "Well, this is like my other two churches: small, family-oriented, humble, but hard working. I know what I am getting into."

Does she? Putting aside for the moment the question of changes in the church's neighborhood, what is Rev. Lovejoy assuming? She is banking on the idea that everything she sees will mean the same thing in the new parish as it did in the former ones. This is a dangerous assumption! She needs to take into account that two other levels of culture are in operation.

The second level is that of *espoused values*. These are beliefs within the church about what is important, what the community says it values. On her first Sunday in the new parish, Rev. Lovejoy might hear several members say to her, "We are a warm and friendly church!" Pastor might take these statements as a good sign. She would figure that this congregation is ready to welcome people from the neighborhood, whose ethnicity is different from its own. For some church members, this might perhaps be the case. However, the statement—as an espoused value—probably means something different. It more than likely refers to the longtime members' friendships within the congregation, the caring and support that they receive from one another. Unless Rev. Lovejoy observes more behavior and asks some careful, but not threatening, questions, she might draw the wrong conclusion.

Similarly, what might Rev. Lovejoy think if, on her first Sunday, she heard two or three older members say, "We liked our other woman minister, so we think that we will like you, too." What is the espoused value here? Tolerance for women in a role with which older members are not fully comfortable? In most organizations, espoused values tend to be expressed in positive terms about features of the group's life that it hopes will come across favorably. Gender inclusion in the pulpit is a change that has been occurring during the lifetime of most adults who were alive during World War II. For many of them, women preachers represent a significant cultural shift. Many will seek to espouse the importance of accepting men or women as pastors. But how can anyone tell if that value has "taken," if it has become embedded in that congregation's culture?

To answer this question, we must consider the third, and most significant, level of culture. It is that of the *shared basic assumptions*. These are the most significant because they define the culture, they reveal what makes it tick. Yet their existence within the particular community is almost subterranean. Shared basic assumptions are not easy to determine; in fact, most longtime members of established congregations are not readily conscious of them. This is not because of something wrong with the members; it is due to the very nature of basic assumptions themselves.

When any community or organization is forming, its members face numerous tasks, both within itself [2] and as it deals with its context.[3] Each time it follows a proposed course of action, to see if it works, the new organization is testing an espoused value. If that course of action appears to the members of the group to have been successful, the particular value will be transformed into a shared, underlying assumption. Thus, one reason that assumptions are difficult to uncover is that the group usually is not able to retain the stories of discussions and events that culminated in its initial success.[4] In the absence of such revealing stories, the assumptions take on a truth within the organization that is unquestioned.

Multiply this course of group learning by the number of tasks and challenges that any new organization faces, and you can begin to get an idea of how complex the culture-forming process becomes. Culture is never as straightforward and apparent as we might suppose it—or wish it—to be. Over the years, a church will have developed a number of shared basic assumptions, and few, if any, of them will be evident to anyone. Yet, try to propose something new, that unknowingly violates one of the assumptions, and you will discover just how powerful cultural assumptions are!

Shared Assumptions in Local Churches

For Rev. Lovejoy, then, her new appointment holds a significant but essential challenge. What are the basic, shared assumptions that lie beneath what the congregation says is important (espoused values) and how the congregation behaves and constructs objects (artifacts)? It is likely that some of the new church's shared assumptions will be similar to those from Rev. Lovejoy's previous parishes. This is the case because many of the sources of shared assumptions will be the same for all three churches (e.g., the national culture, the denomination's general culture, etc.).[5] Rev. Lovejoy will need to be aware, however, that similar-looking artifacts and similar-sounding espoused values do not automatically lead to similar shared assumptions. The idiosyncratic nature of each congregation's particular history means that every church will develop its assumptions in its own distinctive way. At times, a new pastor might feel that assumptions are inscrutable, but they can be decoded, given time and alert observation.

What might a church's set of shared assumptions look like? Below, I suggest several that seem to have been at work in churches that I have served or with which I have had contact. Many of them will appear recognizable in some form to people in many churches; the variations sometimes are only subtle:

"Our church is religious but not fanatical."
"The people with power have been around a long time and have proven themselves."
"We get only so close to our pastors, because they never stay long."
"New people should fit into the old ways."
"Our building contains so many of our precious memories."
"We probably never will be as important as we used to be."
"We make sure that we take care of ourselves first."
"Theology is true only when it is confirmed in our experience."
"Women in our church might not be granted authority, but they definitely exercise power."
"The pastor takes care of the spiritual needs; the members take care of the earthly needs."

As Pastor Lovejoy becomes better acquainted with her new appointment, she gradually will discover shared assumptions like these. They rarely, if ever, will be articulated, unless some action or situation triggers concern within well-established church members. Then one of them, in a moment of anger, frustration, or even fear, might put words to something that all the other longtime members already "know" is "true" for their church. This kind of circumstance is not a pleasant or productive way for a pastor to discover the church's underlying assumptions. Unfortunately, however, it is often the way that many of us have found them out: We run into them, like stepping on a land mine.

THE GOOD NEWS AND THE BAD NEWS

So, then, when it comes to your new church's set of shared assumptions, there is good news and bad news. The good news is that they can be discovered, or decoded, from the artifacts and espoused values. The bad news is that there is probably no way a new pastor can be completely guaranteed of avoiding an unpleasant confrontation with a submerged assumption. Similarly, pastors will learn that some of their church's assumptions have a negative spin to them. Small churches, for instance, who have been on the edge of survival for years, or who have been devastated by conflict, often develop an assumption like, "We will never amount to much or be good at anything." It will take some years of pastoral effort in preaching and pastoral care before the congregation can replace that poor assumption with a constructive one.

Pastors who want to serve their congregations should not despair that the prospect of understanding their flock can get so complicated. If human communities were not so rich and textured, it would not be so. The purpose of discussing these three levels of culture in this first chapter is to set the stage for the pastor's entire tenure with the congregation. Whether you are a candidate for a call or are appointed, there is no way for you to know everything that you need to know about that congregation. Yet you can get started off on the right foot, by taking your need for cultural learning seriously.

In later chapters, we will return to the three levels of culture, as we discuss other topics. For now, we turn to another set of concepts that help us to appreciate the richness that indeed comprises our churches' cultures.

Layers of Culture

Besides thinking of culture in terms of three levels, it is helpful for us to be aware that it exists also in layers.[6] Congregations live in culture that they create, but they don't create culture out of nothing. There are various layers in the church's context, each one functioning as a "host" from which the church unquestioningly draws.[7] These layers usually are invisible and out of consciousness to the church members; like fish in a tank, members don't think about the stuff in which they are swimming.

An easy way to distinguish between levels and layers is that each layer listed below can be broken down into three levels. In other words, *levels* has to do with depth, *layers* with scale. For ease of understanding, I discuss them here from the geographically broadest to the geographically most confined.

Macroculture. In the United States, many congregations display an American flag in their sanctuary. That flag is one of the most prominent symbols of the "macroculture" of the United States. So powerful is that symbolism that many church members would be upset if the flag were absent.

Such was the lesson learned by one young pastor, as the congregation he served was redecorating the sanctuary following a fire. The pastor proposed at the board meeting that a new Christian flag and stand be purchased, but not an American flag. His reasoning was that the church members' loyalty should be first and foremost to Christ, not to a nation or government. That proposal and logic did not sit well with the board members. Most of them had lived through World War II and the Korean War, watching family members and friends serve and die. For them, the American flag symbolized the freedom to worship and loyalty to a country who protected its people and others who were oppressed. The pastor retreated from his proposal, bewildered and wounded in his leadership with the congregation.

What this young pastor did not take into account was the presence of a particular stream of American macroculture in the congregation. Macroculture is that large-scale, national layer in which stories, customs, rituals, heroes, symbols, and the like express what it means to be the United

States of America. One point to realize about this—as with any—layer of culture is that it does not depend on universal agreement. Cultures are created, nurtured, and transmitted without a democratic vote. They emerge from the experience of communities and take on a sense of rightness, even in the face of counterevidence. This point is particularly important to clarify in our post-Civil Rights era, in which the meanings of being American continue to undergo their own cultural change.

In other words, macroculture is real, and it impinges on anyone who steps on United States soil, whether they understand it, like it, want it, seek it, or not. Anyone who has traveled in another country begins to get a sense of the influence of macroculture. Travelers realize that "they don't do everything our way"—macrocultures indeed vary from country to country. The National Anthem; the Constitution; the Civil War; Washington, D.C.; country-western music; and many other artifacts express various aspects of the American way of life. While our cultural interpretation of that way of life can and does change some over time, its presence as macroculture is undeniable.

Our local churches are shaped by American macroculture, as the story above of the American flag so readily illustrates. Because our churches exist in this country and consist primarily of residents and citizens of this country, American macroculture is laced throughout our churches. And because culture itself is composed, not just of the obvious artifacts, but of espoused values and underlying, shared assumptions, the effects of macroculture in our churches are not always evident. Hence, brand-new pastors are wise to become aware of which macro (American)-assumptions most heavily shape the congregation's life.

Mesoculture. Between the grand and sometimes overwhelming realities of macroculture and the singular features of a local culture (see below), we encounter several in-between layers. These "meso" (i.e., "middle") layers are every bit as real as macroculture; and, even though they are independent of one another, they will interact in various ways. In any given location, their presence and effect will vary from church to church. By identifying each of these mesocultures, we can see why this is the case.

Regional. I grew up in a part of the United States that is called, by residents of other parts of the country, "out West." That is not a phrase with which I grew up, however. We thought of ourselves as living in the "Northwest" because that is where we were located when you looked at a map of the United States. In later years, I gradually realized that my part of the country was more easily identifiable if I said I was from the "Pacific Northwest." Apparently, from the perspective of other parts of the nation, there are other "northwests." Why else would "Northwestern University" be located near Chicago? Even the notion of what "west" is depends on your geographical location. My first pastoral position out of seminary was near Denver, which was 1,200 miles east of all the places where I had lived up to that time. What I noticed upon arriving in Colorado, however, were the many signs and references to being in the "far west." "From whose point of view?" I wondered.

These personal musings about geography and perspective begin to point to the cultural phenomenon that I call "regional mesoculture." In the United States, we can observe parts of the country that, for particular purposes, are commonly identified by directional labels—North, South, Midwest, Southwest, Northeast, and so on. If we look more closely, however—by spending time in these various areas—we begin to realize that the geographical distinctions go deeper than the national map. They also represent variations in culture.

Anyone who has traveled in the United States becomes aware, to some degree, of such cultural variations. In every case, idiosyncratic combinations of geography, climate, and immigration/settlement patterns have shaped them. Stereotypes that people in one part of the country hold of those in other parts illustrate some features of regional mesoculture. Easterners are often characterized as being brusque, Southerners as gracious and hospitable, Westerners as independent, and so on. Such characterizations are just the tip of the mesocultural iceberg.

Churches always exist in some regional mesocultural context. I first became aware of some of these differences soon after moving from the Northwest (the "real" one, that is!) to the Midwest to serve a church there. It was summer, hot and muggy as I had never experienced weather before. One of the first church meetings that I attended there was held at night, and I already had deduced that those attending would be free to dress casually. Fortunately, the office where we met had air conditioning. I wore a casual shirt with a collar, cotton slacks, and sandals with bare feet. The other men in attendance were wearing similar shirts and slacks. Later, however, I found out that the sandals and bare feet made a big impression—the wrong kind! It had not occurred to me that my Western way of staying comfortable would be viewed in my new location as inappropriate. Some kind of shared assumption was at work among them, one that was different from anything to which I had been accustomed.

Pastors who labor in a call system are more likely to move to different parts of the country than are pastors who are appointed year after year to parishes in the same conference. Consequently, called pastors are more likely to bump into mesocultural assumptions that are new, unfamiliar, and even seemingly odd. If we grew up mainly in one region of the country, we will have been shaped by the shared assumptions of that region. It takes time to get accustomed to artifacts and espoused values that are distinct. It takes even more time, as well as careful attention, to be aware of the underlying assumptions.

Regional mesoculture is only one kind of mesoculture. There are others, and most of them have little to do with geography. The one exception is related to geography in a different way.

Racial/ethnic. Virtually all metropolitan areas in the United States have at least one thing in common: Their populations hail from a variety of places. Visit today's American city, ride its buses and trains, stroll its streets, walk the halls of its schools, and you will encounter people whose origins link them to places all around the world. Being American gradually is becoming less and less a Caucasian phenomenon; we are now less like a melting pot and more like a salad bowl.

This increasing racial and ethnic diversity brings another dimension to the richness of mesoculture. It means that no matter whether you are in Chicago, Los Angeles, or Atlanta, pockets of a variety of ethnic life and expression thrive. Mexican, German, African American, Irish, South Indian, Korean, and many other communities with roots elsewhere are now also here. Because culture is so tenacious, all these ethnic groups—especially those newest to the United States—maintain many aspects of their native culture. We could identify these racial/ethnic mesocultures anywhere in the United States, regardless of their exact location.

It is not insignificant to recognize that virtually all racial/ethnic mesocultures in the United States were—or are—macrocultures in their homelands. Artifacts, espoused values, and underlying assumptions, with strong histories in native soil, should not be expected to disappear easily in a new context. For whatever reasons that people emigrate to the United States, their culture comes with them. That culture adapts to its new surroundings as it provides security and meaning to those who bear and transmit it.

One primary reason that established churches in communities where ethnicity is changing have a hard time surviving is due to the power of mesocultures. It is not easy for aging members of a declining church to generate the energy—let alone the appropriate insights—that it would take to be effectively hospitable to a new ethnic group. Acknowledging this difficulty does not, however, categorically dismiss the potential for developing authentic cross-cultural ministry out of a transition. The point is, rather, that simply being earnest and devout about reaching out probably will not get very far. In this context, mesoculture will be the key to communicating and relating effectively.

In our opening story of the chapter, Pastor Johnson did not manage to learn enough of Chinese American mesoculture to be perceived by the members as effective for their congregation. Nor did the congregation find a way to convey to her the deeply shaped assumptions about pastor-parish relations in a Chinese mesoculture. Christians seeking to extend hospitality to a different ethnic group must be prepared to learn many things. Anthony Gittins's book, *Gifts and Strangers*, provides the kind of insightful resources for such a task.[8] In the next chapter, we will see how Gittins's analysis of cross-cultural mission work also helps us understand what I call the pastor's experience of "adoption."

Class. In the United States, economics has some influence on culture, too. Most of us familiar with the popular media are accustomed to hearing such phrases as "lower class," "working class," "middle class," "affluent," "wealthy," "old money," and so on. Such terms help us distinguish between ways of life that are related to the level of material resources to which a person has access. At the same time, though, investments and annual income alone are insufficient ways to decipher a culture. The term, "class," then, becomes yet another way to recognize certain cultural distinctions, this time apart from reference to a specific location.

Think, for instance, about all the suburban communities you have seen in your lifetime. After a while, it does not matter much whether you are driving through Alabama or Alaska: There are many features of suburban life that will appear pretty much the same in any state. The kinds of houses, yards, automobiles, clothing, and social activities preferred by suburbia's residents comprise some of its artifacts. This general comparison also can be made between other class-related communities across various regions of the United States. I noticed these kinds of similarities, for instance, in small towns and rural areas of southern Oregon and "downstate" (i.e., away from Chicago) Illinois. Men in both places often wore brimmed caps, faded plaid shirts, blue jeans, and boots and drove dirt-splattered pickup trucks while listening to country-western music and chewing tobacco. My point is not that everyone who lives in similar mesocultures is exactly the same, but that artifacts like these do symbolize an outdoor, working-class culture. What these communities have in common, despite being separated by thousands of miles, in many ways is more significant than what differs because of region.

Class, then, helps create another of our American mesocultures. The effects of class mesoculture on pastoral attitudes appear evident, once we begin to reflect on some commonly accepted patterns of pastoral movement. Many seminary-educated pastors would choose to serve a congregation in a thriving suburb or city neighborhood. Parallel to the corporate model, pastors and denominations often regard a pastoral career as one of "climbing the ladder." Supposedly, we pastors expect over the years to move to larger, more prestigious congregations, to positions with more authority and larger compensation packages. I am claiming that this expectation does indeed reveal a particular bias toward one kind of class mesoculture over another. The issues run much deeper than financial, geographical, or social; they have to do with a way of life, with culture. In order for us to appreciate how class affects the way that pastors get along with churches, one aspect of this layer should be explored a little further.

Traditional Orality. One class of mesoculture in particular calls for separate attention because pastors, denominations, and seminaries tend to misunderstand it. This mesoculture is most evident in rural, small-town, working-class communities across the United States. It has been described and interpreted very effectively by Tex Sample, most notably in his short but revelatory work, *Ministry in an Oral Culture.*[9]

Sample claims that, in spite of all its interest in formal education and professionalism, American society continues to be deeply infused by a way of life that is by nature primarily oral. This way of life, though varying in details of custom from place to place, relies heavily on long-standing relationships and a sense of location and tradition. Its lifeblood is best expressed by the ancient practices of telling stories and coining wisdom sayings or proverbs. Its people learn best through memorization and apprenticeship, reflecting on life not in abstract terms but based in their own particular experiences. It is less program- than gathering-oriented, using gift exchange as a means for expressing both appreciation and obligation. Sample calls this way of life "traditional orality" or "oral culture."[10]

Having grown up with oral culture all around me, I found Sample's explanations both constructive and convicting. I have had to reassess my judgmental attitudes about communities who were not interested in my "literate culture" preference for analytical thought, politically correct causes, and classical music. The people who comprise oral culture, Sample contends, add up to half of the population in the United States—notably higher outside of Western countries. Local church memberships are more likely than not to be heavily influenced by traditions and practices from oral culture.[11] This will be true whether considering a country church or a blue-collar parish in the city.

The implications of these claims could lead to a paradigm shift of its own for pastoral leadership and administration. For our purposes here, we need to recognize traditional orality as a *bona fide* mesoculture. Instead of trying to avoid it, those of us who are both called to ministry and are well educated would do well to learn to appreciate orality on its own terms. Realistically, pastors in appointment traditions will serve amidst oral culture people not infrequently. Just as realistically, pastors in call traditions will be taken by surprise if they do not or will not, in any given congregation, account for the presence and particular potential of oral culture.

Generational. Last but not least, our American society experiences cultural distinctions that occur as a result of differences between generations. All of us have heard such terms as "baby boomers" and "Generation X" used in the popular media. What came to be known as "the generation gap" in the 1960s is now analyzed by some theorists in a much broader framework of historical and social context.[12] According to these theories, all the people born within a certain twenty-year time span share a number of characteristics in common. These characteristics emerge as a result of that particular generation's place in historical events and social dynamics. Some theorists even argue that patterns of such characteristics repeat themselves every four generations in the United States. William Strauss and Neil Howe name the generations as follows:

IDEALIST: spiritual, narcissistic, moralistic, and visionary (boomers)
REACTIVE: criticized, alienated, pragmatic, and reclusive (Xers)
CIVIC: achieving, building, and busy (GIs)
ADAPTIVE: suffocated, conformist, indecisive, and sensitive (silent
   majority) [13]

Each generation in the cycle develops a "mood" that stays with it, taking different forms as new generations emerge behind it. Generational theory, according to its proponents, helps to explain many of the differences of value, behavior, and preferences between age groups. Boomers who mystified their parents with tie-dyed shirts, rock music, and free love have experienced mystification with their own children's styles of dress, music, and social activities.

One of the most suggestive indications of the effect of generational difference upon churches is the relatively low ratio of boomers who attend church.

Their parents were optimistic that they would return to church when they became parents, but research reveals otherwise.[14] Debate continues among many denominational groups, for instance, whether boomers and their children would be attracted to a church that put aside formal worship and old hymns for informality and contemporary music.

If, as a pastor, older members of your congregation ever have told you that they wanted to attract more young people, you might not have realized that you were in danger of stepping on a land mine! Persons who have been in churches virtually all of their adult lives realize that younger people eventually must replace them. In a society in which church participation is voluntary, however, the difficult question that any aging congregation must ask itself is, "Why would anyone want to join us?" This question, if taken seriously, will force churches to think hard about constructively negotiating differences between their generation and the ones behind them.

Microculture. Perhaps all this delineation of cultural categories on such broad scales seems a bit abstract. What to some might feel more real about culture is its immediate impact in a concrete, local setting. Most of us live most of our lives in such local settings—towns, cities, rural counties, and so on. Culture develops a special character in settings such as these. This layer of culture is called "micro" because of the smaller scale compared to the others discussed earlier. The specific circumstances, persons, opportunities, major events, and so forth give every microculture its distinctiveness.

I have lived in small towns, rural areas, small cities, and neighborhoods of large cities. In each of these demographic contexts, I became aware of something of the idiosyncratic nature of the microculture. While some of the artifacts and espoused values were quite similar among them all, each place gradually would reveal something about itself that was peculiar. "Peculiar" does not necessarily mean odd or negative, but rather distinctive. These peculiar elements are the most challenging for an outsider to learn and decipher, but they are the ones that help a pastor in a new setting to get the lay of the land.

We have spent some time in this chapter defining a number of concepts that help elaborate on the rich notion of culture. The three levels and five layers that we have discussed here could seem confusing. If they do, I am contending that it is only because the phenomena that we are attempting to understand are themselves so nuanced and complex. Before we tie all this discussion more explicitly to cultural capital and how pastors learn about new churches, let us meet one more concept. This notion already was implied as we introduced microculture. Aspects of macroculture and various mesocultures all meet in certain ways in microculture. That kind of coming together is what I call "confluence."

CULTURAL CONFLUENCE

Why should all these concepts describing various aspects of culture be important to pastors? The answer to this question is, I believe, deceptively simple. It is because any one parish or congregation is like a specific intersection of all these levels and layers. In other words, when you are preparing to enter a congregation for the first time, you are walking into a stream of culture that is created out of many other streams. It is the confluence of all the many idiosyncratic elements that meet in that one church in that certain way that makes each church distinctive. It is the reality of the confluence of cultural streams that makes church analysis possible—albeit subtle and challenging.

The impact of cultural confluence in a congregation might appear more dramatic in those churches (often few and far between) where the artifacts of diversity are most evident. We would become much more conscious of confluence if we observed a worship service that included virtually all ages, with persons from several ethnic groups and races, singing and listening to music from America, Africa, and Asia, including in the liturgy both contemplative and expressive rituals of participation.

Theoretically, this kind of worship is possible; it requires deliberate attention to cultural particularities that rarely blend together smoothly in daily life. Instead, most of our churches express a religious culture informed by a more defined, and confined, set of traditions. Especially when we are accustomed to one way of "being church," it becomes more difficult for us to isolate what originally was more of a plethora of cultural streams. Of course, worship is not the only place in a church's life where confluence occurs; we sense its presence as well in fellowship, educational activities, church business, and the like.

Once we learn to watch for it, we will see confluence in every congregation. Elements of American macroculture join with elements from the regional mesoculture, the particular blend of racial-ethnic mesoculture, the cultural class of the church's founders, as well as the values and moods of each successive generation. Every church has its own unique blend of culture, based on these many sources converging in that spot. Being in a church is quite an experience—especially if we know what we are looking for.

THE NOTION OF CULTURAL CAPITAL

In this chapter, we are exploring what it takes for pastors who enter a new parish—either by appointment or by call—to understand their new situation. Our goal is to recognize the tremendous influence of culture on the effectiveness of such understanding. The several terms that have been introduced here serve to underscore the importance of culture, by giving us conceptual tools for insight.

All these conceptual tools converge when we begin to think about "cultural capital." This phrase is a metaphor, since, strictly speaking, there is no money or other tangible commodity involved in the way culture is lived out. At the same time, though, applying the notion of capital to culture opens up some significant insights about how culture looks, acts, and feels.

Consider this contrast: A pastor who has served a congregation for twenty years; who has baptized, married, buried, and wept with its members; who has designed and led seasons of worship that uplift and strengthen; who has taught and encouraged learning; who has been a voice of hope in crisis and a voice of action in need is a pastor with a lot of cultural capital. On the other hand, the pastor who has just completed theological training; who has been appointed to his or her first parish; who is known by few other pastors in the conference and no one in the new parish is a pastor with a lot of work to do. It is not merely the passage of time that helps a pastor develop cultural capital. Rather, it is when, however consciously or intuitively, she or he both understands and is received by the congregation, that the accrual of a pastor's cultural capital will begin to pay off in ministry.

Whether a bishop, a cabinet, or a search committee determines a pastorate, eventually all pastors must come to terms with the congregations they actually encounter. Learning to get along, so as to thrive in gospel ministry, is not necessarily easy. That is why this chapter has avoided simplistic answers or quip-like proverbs in laying a foundation for knowing what you are getting into. The characteristics and realities that the concepts in this chapter identify set the stage for the intricate drama that constitutes your church.

PREPARING TO KNOW YOUR NEW PARISH

Let us now focus on what pastors can do to ready themselves to enter a new parish. We will keep in mind the levels and layers of culture as we frame the issues in these rich yet subtle terms. There are preparations that you can make by yourself, before and during the process, in which you acquire information about the new church from available sources.

FOR YOURSELF

If you serve by appointment, you might enter a situation in which most of your gathered knowledge about the new parish comes through word-of-mouth. What does the bishop tell you about the church and, if anything, why is she or he sending you there? What information can be shared appropriately through a presiding elder, district superintendent, cabinet member, or like official? Do you know other pastors who have served there? What can they tell you? By chance, do you know any of the church members, and what can they share about life there? What is the reputation of this parish in your conference?

If you are able to cull information from all the sources listed above, you will have a bounty of information indeed. The deeper question, however, is, "What does all this mean?" This is your first, and ongoing, task. Most of what you hear about the new charge will reveal many of the church's artifacts and even some of its espoused values. As we noted earlier, these two levels of culture are the most evident, but not the most important. It is the shared assumptions that are symbolized through the artifacts (and partially—yes, even inconsistently—revealed through the espoused values) that you eventually must decode. The time needed for such decoding is longer than the time it takes to leave the annual conference and move into the parsonage! So, in one sense, you will be decoding for the entire duration of your appointment, especially the shorter it is.

Don't allow this reality to discourage you. Congregations with appointed pastors are used to them being "clueless." The advantage that you will have is in knowing that what you see is not all of what you will get. You will enter this charge in a much stronger position to begin discerning where the culture that you bring both converges and diverges from the congregation's. So secondly, make mental notes of these differences from the very beginning. Note also what you do not yet know; this will apply especially to the congregation's history and its story, as well as its day-to-day, weekly, and monthly rhythms.

It would be a grave mistake on your part to conclude that any of the church's differences from your "style" should be immediately changed. A new pastor does not build cultural capital by behaving in ways that dishonor the parish's own culture. You might discover that you have to add a new sentence to your church vocabulary: "I'm sorry; I am still new, and I didn't realize what I was doing." This is not a sign of weakness but of wisdom.

Third, assess how you will have to adjust your special skills and interests. Remember that your goal is to build capital by honoring something that you are still learning. Your previous church might have established a highly successful day care center under your leadership. Do not assume that your new parish has "day care" on its cultural radar, regardless of what you perceive to be the community's need for one. Instead, ask yourself, "What will it take for this congregation to see that I seek to meet them in their world? How can I do that, in worship, in preaching, in fellowship contacts, in groups and auxiliaries, and in the way that business is conducted?" This is what

Massey and McKinney's story in the preface means about "backing up and hooking up" before you pull out of the station.

For those in the search and call process, you might have received a copy of a church profile or information form, providing standardized data about the congregation, its community, and expectations for ministry with its new pastor. What do these data tell you, so that you can decide whether to pursue the process? Being artifacts sprinkled with a few espoused values, the profile data suggest some things about the congregation's culture. How can you find out more?

You are in the position of being able to seek information from more than one source: from the search committee itself; from the denominational official who assists in calls; from other pastors or persons who know the congregation. What will you ask them?

It might sound as though I am implying that pastors in call systems automatically know what they are getting into better than those in appointments. This is not necessarily true, though having the opportunity to say "yes" or "no" at least gives the appearance of a favorable vantage point. If nothing else, calls at least might be able to provide the new pastor with a bit of a head start. The key is whether, during the candidacy process, the pastor searches for the right kinds of insights. Such insights will point to some of the congregation's espoused values and, one would hope, a few of its shared assumptions.

QUESTIONS TO USE WITH OTHERS

As you either enter or consider a new church, the knowledge and insights of people who know that church can help you. The following questions are designed to be worded appropriately for different parties. That is, when you inquire of others about this church, you want to avoid sounding judgmental, prying, or too self-assured. Some of the questions in the different categories below are similar to others, but are phrased differently for the sake of impact. Your purpose is to get enough information about this church's confluence of cultures, its artifacts, and espoused values so that you can begin to understand what you are getting into.

To the bishop, presiding elder, or district superintendent:

- Have you worked with this parish on any issues, difficult or otherwise? What can you share of the outcome?
- How has this parish treated its last few pastors? What do they say they want from the office of pastor?
- What are one or two major episodes in this church's life that are still remembered? Do you know why these remain in its corporate memory?
- What new idea might this church be most willing to try? Least willing?
- What do you see as this congregation's greatest need right now? Its best opportunity for ministry?

For those in call processes, to outsiders who know the congregation:

- What would be typical kinds of comments or statements that members of this congregation might make:

  in worship?
  at a board meeting?
  during a fellowship event?
  to a next-door neighbor?

- Who are the key influential members? What are their interests for the congregation?
- What "shadows" in the congregation's past might help explain something important about it today?

For the pastor search committee:

- What is the day-to-day life of the church like?
- How do the various committees and auxiliaries feel about each other?
- Explain how the search committee came to list these particular expectations of the pastor.
- What do these pastoral expectations say about the congregation itself?
- If your pastor did something that did not "fit in," who in the church would be concerned, and why?

To both outsiders to the church and the search committee:

- What has life in this church been like over the last ten years?
- What events and incidents have shaped this congregation to become what it is?
- What do members like to do for fun? Are there different segments of the church who have various interests?
- What language does the congregation use to describe itself?
- How much variation from different routines is the congregation willing to try?

Entering the world of a new parish can be both exciting and frustrating. It is possible, if we use effective tools, to increase the excitement variable in the equation and reduce the frustration variable. A culture model like the one outlined in this chapter serves as one such tool. With it, our transition as new pastor can go smoother. Who knows? We might even get adopted by the congregation! The importance of pastoral adoption is the subject of the next chapter.

"Welcome to the Family!"

Have You Been Adopted Yet?

WHISTLE-BLOWING THAT BACKFIRED

R EV. JONES LOOKED FORWARD to his next pastorate. He was an experienced pastor—talented, outgoing, energetic, supportive, and full of ideas. St. James was a large congregation, in a modest but comfortable suburb, with resources to do many things. On the day that he was elected pastor, several members said to him afterward, "We are used to our pastors staying a long time. We hope that you will stay twenty years!"

Five years went by. Things between Rev. Jones and St. James seemed to be going well: Church participation continued strong, financial giving was up, and ministry was expanding. Then Rev. Jones discovered something that he at first could not believe. The congregation's longtime treasurer, a highly regarded member of the church, had been embezzling church funds. It was a large amount of money, equal to half the church's annual operating budget. Pastor Jones was stunned but, since no one else apparently had yet come upon the predicament, he decided that he had a responsibility to the church to take action. Keeping his knowledge from the treasurer, the pastor called together some key elected church officials and discussed what to do. Rev. Jones recommended a plan of action to which the church's officials agreed, though reluctantly. The police were called in, the treasurer was confronted and confessed, he was arrested and taken to jail.

Six months later, Rev. Jones was looking for another pastorate. The treasurer's arrest created a furor in the congregation. Active church members who had been friendly and supportive of Rev. Jones now would not speak to him. He even received a few threats of violence. So he worked out terms of a severance package with the congregation and began circulating his dossier.

"ARE YOU ONE OF US?"

What had happened at St. James Church to spoil what appeared to be a mutually beneficial, noteworthy relationship between pastor and parish? How could a congregation so suddenly and vindictively turn against its pastor? Was there any way for Pastor Jones to be aware ahead of time that he was stepping on one of St. James's land mines? Who had the "right" to act as they did: the pastor, in trying to protect the church's financial security, or the church, in forcing the pastor to quit? Or does asking about "right" and "wrong" ever lead us to the kind of insight from which we can learn something about getting along with churches?

As is the case with many poignant stories from parishes, this one about Rev. Jones and the embezzled church is pregnant with many lessons. In chapter 4, for instance, we will discuss the pastor's role in helping the congregation deal with hard issues and crises. In this regard, Rev. Jones clearly was not successful, despite his good intentions. Yet, for the purposes of this chapter, I want to draw our attention to a different aspect of the pastor-parish challenge. This aspect is the next major issue that a pastor needs to address in order to get along with the church. Experienced pastors know this issue from proverbial sayings passed on to them in their early years— sayings like, "You've got to pay your dues first" or "The congregation has to accept you before any real ministry can happen." From the congregation's standpoint, the issue might be articulated, if at all, through the question, "Are you one of us?"

In this chapter, the question of a pastor coming to "belong" to the congregation—of fitting in, being known and knowing, of dues-paying and being accepted—will be framed in the metaphor of adoption. As you might expect, our perspective on adoption will be cultural. That is, we will frame it in light of the experience of the congregation as a community, and of the mysterious dance that begins when a pastor arrives to join that community. Unlike actual adoption into a family unit, pastoral adoption cannot be orchestrated in some legal, formal way. It occurs instead at some practically incalculable *kairos*, that blessed moment in their relationship when the pastor's way of being with the people symbolizes what they expect and hope.

Because this book seeks to build on a cognitive interpretive framework and not simply anecdotal wisdom, pastoral adoption can be understood somewhat technically. Our understanding of it will be built on the cultural capital perspective that we began to frame in chapter 1. In the language of the levels of culture, adoption occurs when the pastor uses the congregation's artifacts to symbolize its shared assumptions in a way that the church can affirm is important to the members (espoused values). This statement summarizes what it "looks like" for the pastor to establish some cultural capital.

BIBLICAL STRANGERS AND ADOPTION

The notion of adoption appears in a number of passages in the Bible. One of the most famous, of course, occurs when the Hebrew baby Moses is cast afloat among the bulrushes in Egypt, to be discovered by pharaoh's daughter and subsequently raised as her son (Exod. 2:1–10). Here, adoption becomes a fascinating linchpin in the story of the Israelites. As a young man, Moses flees pharaoh's house after killing an Egyptian, marries a shepherd's daughter (another kind of adoption), and settles down for what he must have thought would be a tough but quiet life. We know that is not how the story works out! Another key adoption of sorts takes place in the story of Ruth, the Moabite woman who stays with Naomi, her mother-in-law, after both of their husbands die (the well-known "whither thou goest, I will go . . . " passage [Ruth 1:16–17]). Naomi then helps Ruth find another husband, Boaz. Their marriage yields a son, Obed, who turns out to be the grandfather of the great King David. Jesus, you remember, was born from the house of David (Matt. 1:1–17; Luke 1:26–33).

Adoption also plays a part in the theology of the New Testament. The term is used to explain one of the results of Christian salvation, as in Romans 8. Here, Paul is discussing a completion of God's full purposes for all creation (vv. 18–25). In the "present time" (v. 18), believers yearn to be adopted by God as an indication of that fullness (v. 23). Elsewhere, adoption is used as one of several metaphors for reconciliation between Jews and Gentiles. Ephesians speaks of how the blood of Christ has "brought near" those who were once far off (2:13). Besides using the images of "citizens" (v. 19), "holy temple" (v. 21), and "dwelling place" (v. 22), this passage also speaks of Gentile believers as "members of the household of God" (v. 19). Thus, the very early church experienced bonding across traditional lines; it was the kind of bonding that reminded them of adoption.

These biblical references carry implications with significant application to pastors in new churches. Both Moses and Ruth—not to mention the Gentile Christians served by Paul's ministry—originally were strangers to the community. Except in cases in which a grown child succeeds his or her parent as pastor of a congregation, pastors today indeed arrive, most of the time, as strangers to their new churches. As we will further see below, the status of stranger is a marginal one. There is a sense in which that marginality never completely goes away, even when a pastor is adopted. We need to explore this point later. Before we do so, let us develop this practical notion of adoption.

Anthony Gittins's anthropological insights about missionaries and strangers can be applied readily to pastors and their new churches: Pastors are strangers to a new community that must find a way to welcome them.[1] We will use some of Gittins's material to explore the intricacies of a pastor's becoming adopted by a congregation.

STRANGERS AND HOSTS

A missionary, like a new pastor, enters new territory and a new people who inhabit it. The missionary (pastor) arrives there as a stranger and must learn to get along with the hosts. Gittins is helpful in pointing out that there are several dynamics involved for both stranger (pastor) and host (new congregation).[2] The host community technically is the one in charge, for it is the one on whom the stranger must depend—and in traditional missionary terms, this is often literally the case. If the stranger (pastor) shows her or his willingness to accept this position of deference to the host (new church), the relationship gets off on the right foot.

At this point, then, the host (new church) must accept responsibility to extend hospitality to the stranger (pastor). As Gittins says, something of a status change must be effected, which must be initiated by the host (new church): "Just as it takes a host to make a stranger, so it takes a host to make a guest."[3] At the same time, however, hosts expect something in return. They expect their stranger/guest (pastor) to allow them to institute this status change, by respectfully negotiating it in the terms of the hosts (new church). Failure on the part of the stranger/guest to do so, whether unintentional or otherwise, taxes the host's forbearance and concern for safekeeping. This is why strangers (new pastors) can rightly expect a certain element of trepidation and ambivalence among their hosts. Relationships are bound up with trust and the sharing of hospitality, which easily can be damaged by the stranger/guest (pastor).

There are things to which the stranger/guest therefore must attend. She or he must realize that entering the world of the host involves taking on a posture of learning and an ability to be uncomfortable at times. The stranger/guest (pastor) is the object of the host's (new church's) hospitality; she or he must receive the hospitality that is offered, recognizing that it comes in the forms of the unfamiliar host. Receiving hospitality smoothes the way toward the stranger/guest's (pastor's) adoption. It even can open up the host to the resources that the stranger/guest could provide. For the stranger herself, in arriving from somewhere else, brings a variety of assets that could benefit the host (new church). Such resources remain only potential, until "the establishment of reciprocal relationships"[4] makes further exchange possible. At this point, the stranger/guest (pastor) begins to use some of the cultural capital that he or she has accrued with the host (new church).

Yet, the stranger must continue to be mindful that the host community still views her or him—to some degree—as an outsider. I once served a small-town church with a long history and an aging membership. One of the most active persons in the church was an energetic, retired woman, who taught church school, took kids on trips, cooked in the kitchen, and helped with the annual clean-up day. In a conversation with me, she once revealed, "My husband and I have lived here for forty years, and we're still considered outsiders!" If someone like this can still be tagged "alien," how much more can such a status be applied to the congregation's pastor.

THE ADOPTION/ASSIMILATION PROCESS[5]

Gittins's discussion of the stranger includes a summary of the classic three-stage process of becoming assimilated into a new community.[6] This process easily translates for pastors entering new churches; it is a thumbnail sketch of what it takes to get adopted. First, the stranger begins a preliminary stage that involves being announced, introduced, ceremonially checked out, and even seemingly disgraced. Once the stranger (pastor) "passes" through these steps, then the most trying part of the preliminary stage begins: that of simply "being there" with the host (new church). This part of the experience can be undefined; the stranger will not have much of a sense of what is going on. At this point, assimilation has entered its second stage, the transitional one. The new relationship will seem confusing to the stranger (pastor). Perhaps gifts will come her/his way; perhaps his/her standing changes a bit. It will take patience, adaptability, and persistence for the stranger to move through this threshold experience successfully.

Assuming that the stranger is indeed patient and flexible, going with the flow of action and activity initiated by the host, then the third stage of assimilation, incorporation, will occur. Gittins emphasizes that incorporation is not automatic; the stranger cannot assume that it will be a "done deal." In the metaphor of chapter 1, entering new pastoral territory is like walking across a field of land mines: If you don't know where to step, you just might set off an explosion that will hurt you. Rather, the achievement of impromptu and trustworthy, mutual interchange between stranger (pastor) and host (new church) is reached as the host is persuaded that the stranger can fit in. The stranger cannot and does not initiate incorporation but clearly must be engaging the host appropriately, in order to become incorporated.

Furthermore, this inherently unequal relationship calls for the stranger's support and loyalty of the host.[7] The capacity to question the activities of the host community is not granted through incorporation; it might never be explicitly sought by the host. Remember that the vantage point of the host (new church) must be of paramount consideration to the stranger (pastor) seeking to be incorporated. It is much less a matter of whether the stranger likes what she or he sees than it is in realizing one's precarious standing as a stranger. If the goal is adoption for the sake of deeper ministry, then during assimilation, the stranger sometimes might have to bite his or her tongue.

ST. JAMES AND REV. JONES

Rev. Jones's departure from St. James Church causes us to wonder if he had been adopted or not. We might suppose that five years would have been a long enough period of time for a pastor to be received and assimilated by the congregation. Without having observed the congregation, or interviewed members, we can only guess. However, we definitely can see, perhaps more clearly now, how Rev. Jones violated his stranger/guest status with his host. In retrospect, we can surmise that his handling of the treasurer's embezzlement was like stepping on a land mine in the field of that parish's shared assumptions. It appears as though Jones's actions were interpreted by key culture bearers as something that their church did not allow pastors to do. Jones himself admitted later that he did not become aware very early of the clan relationships among a number of the older families and members.

Jones's whistle-blowing was a symbolic, dramatic act. To the dominant subculture in the congregation, it seems to have signaled a lack of loyalty to the host.[8] There undoubtedly were members of the congregation, newer to the life of that faith community, who disagreed with the decision for Jones's departure. To those who were most strongly aligned to the church's culture, Jones's act was one of criticism, perhaps even of treason. Whether or not he had been adopted before the embezzlement was discovered, Rev. Jones quickly lost that status.

ORAL CULTURE AND ADOPTION

One way to illustrate how important the pastor's adoption is to effective ministry in the congregation is to see how it does—or does not—occur in churches in which oral culture prevails. Traditionally oral congregations reveal the difficulty that seminary-trained pastors face. By the time a person has completed college and graduate theological school, she or he has been enculturated into a way of life very different from traditional orality.

Included in this enculturation is an implicit disdain for the seemingly simpler folkways of rural, small-town, and working-class communities.[9] Highly educated people often lose touch with the cultural power of long-standing relationships, of commitment to a place, of storytelling and proverbs, and of the practices of recall, apprenticeship, and concrete thinking.[10]

What, then, is likely to happen to the "well-educated," but insensitive, pastor who is called or appointed to an oral culture congregation? (By the way, this scenario might be more of a risk for appointed pastors than for those in call traditions.) She or he very well would suppose that many of the church's usual, folksy activities were a waste of time and irrelevant to "real ministry." He or she might attempt to make the church's organizational structure function more efficiently, with regular printed agendas, strict adherence to *Robert's Rules of Order*, attendance policies for elected officers, and the like. She or he might ignore the relationships already established in the congregation and try to create something new by playing members off one another. And, perhaps worst of all, he or she might feel "led by God" to preach to the congregation about everything that she or he saw was "wrong" with the church.

This pastor will not get adopted. Rather than honoring the congregation's members with behavior that supports who they are, this pastor instead would have shamed them. He or she would have conveyed the belief that their artifacts and assumptions were inferior and needed replacing. As a result, he or she would have cut off access to sources of cultural capital. The transitional stage of assimilation will not be navigated. Thus, any chance for that pastor to help the congregation maintain strong ministry or develop further ministry would be soundly lost.

Pastors who are not familiar with oral culture, or who seek to demean its value, are in serious danger of not getting adopted in traditional settings. Their understanding of culture needs to expand. They need to learn to "get inside of" the oral culture of their churches, to come to appreciate those artifacts and espoused values, and to decode the shared assumptions. Let us look briefly at how a sympathetic approach to an oral culture church might enhance one's chances of being adopted.

TIPS FOR TRADITIONAL ADOPTION

First, the new pastor in a traditional-oral church would make it a top priority to learn the congregation and its particular web of connections. This goal recognizes that, in oral culture, these associations and the history that created them constitute so much of what makes the church what it is. Finding out about this web, secondly, should draw the new pastor into the stories that live within the congregation. Astute attention to the stories, and to the telling of them, alerts the new pastor to some of the congregation's espoused values. Meanings that might have been implicit in other corners of the church become more evident through its stories. Third, those "pearls of wisdom" that are shared in members' conversations suggest the church's store of proverbial knowledge. Characters in the James Herriot series of veterinary life in the moors of Scotland often faced struggles and setbacks by saying, "Aye; these things happen." So, also, the oral church shares such sayings.

A new pastor in an oral church can build on these three sources of cultural knowledge in order to make the transition into being adopted. For instance, he or she can use stories and proverbial sayings. The sincere use of a proverb that the pastor has heard among the congregation, if offered in an appropriate setting, symbolizes a growing understanding and appreciation of the people. Stories and proverbs can be very powerful tools in the pastor's preaching and teaching. Many books of the Bible employ stories and proverbs. A culturally alert pastor can become quite adept in keeping abstract ideas to a minimum, building instead on and with the stories and proverbs themselves.

A pastor's cultural capital for adoption in an oral-culture church is also enhanced through the pastor's promotion of memory and recall. Observe how the congregation's regular worship proceeds. See how educational programs function. How can you as the new pastor strengthen (and thus honor) the use of recitation, for instance? How can memory work be utilized creatively, both with children and adults?

Before there were accredited schools and training programs, traditional cultures raised up their workers through apprenticeship. Oral-culture congregations teach their members by involving them in various ways—in leading music, singing in choirs, teaching classes, helping with church meals, maintaining the facilities, and so on. Where are the openings in the congregation's life that you as the new pastor can give members further hands-on experience? Is it in an area that they will accept as open to them? Who are the likely candidates? How do you get them started and encourage them as they participate?

These suggestions and questions are the kinds that will aid the new pastor in a traditionally oral congregation. They can be effective because they grow out of the kind of culture that is already in the church. By approaching pastoral tasks in this way, a new pastor stands a better chance of navigating the transitional stage of adoption by the congregation. She or he will be working with, rather than appearing at odds with, the church's artifacts, espoused values, and shared assumptions. The host/church will be pleased to see their stranger/pastor honoring their way of life. Adoption should happen more smoothly this way. Then the pastor will be in a stronger position to help the congregation respond to opportunities that it previously might not have perceived or interpreted favorably. With enough cultural capital, a pastor can "get away" with more risk taking.

ORALITY IN CONTEXT

Actually, there are elements of oral-culture churches that other church cultures ignore to their peril. In spite of high levels of education, income, sophisticated civic and political involvement, even "well-heeled" churches could stand a good story or two now and then. That is to say, the appeal of narrative is not confined to one kind of community—story invokes all sorts of feelings with all sorts of people. A preacher who does not illustrate a sermon's message with stories or story-like images is not helping the hearers make crucial associations with real life. Church study groups who talk only in abstract terms about their subject matter, without grounding the conversation in actual and personal human experience, cannot move from merely "hearing" to "doing." As James says (1:23–24), they see themselves in a mirror and then depart, "immediately forget[ing] what they were like." Indeed, a congregation that cannot tell its own story and explore new meanings from it is a church that is dying.

So there is value for the parish itself when its new pastor is adopted. He or she is in a better position to use the congregation's culture—that idiosyncratic configuration of cultural confluences—to strengthen its mission. Story is one significant example of how this can occur; there are others, as the discussion above suggests. Let us conclude this part of our exploration of adoption by making one further point explicit: There are elements of oral culture in all other cultures, and pastors are foolish to ignore them. It is one opportunity during the adoption/assimilation process for the pastor to draw on the power of oral features such as story. This practice not only will help symbolize important links in the stranger/host relationship, but it also will prepare the congregation spiritually and missionally. After all, new pastors sometimes are necessary for a church's health; as Gittins puts it, "strangers may actually be necessary for a society to flourish."[11]

SUBCULTURES AND ADOPTION

WHAT ADOPTION IS NOT

Yet, the plot thickens. We need to be clear what adoption does and does not entail. As we have seen already, it does not mean that the pastor becomes fully part of the community. Total assimilation can occur in certain circumstances, such as with a pastor who stays more than a generation in one congregation and becomes the symbol of itself, or with a founding pastor who stays long enough to embed within that nascent congregation a set of shared assumptions.[12] For most churches of our day, however, the culture has developed to the point that the membership does not look for its pastor to be fully "one of us." As we have suggested and will explore in further detail later, this partial marginality is necessary for the good of the congregation.

Adoption also does not mean that the new pastor has won the unwavering approval of every single person in the congregation. The purpose of getting adopted is not for the pastor to win a church popularity contest unanimously! This way of thinking is misleading and actually would undermine chances for an effective adoption to come about. In order to understand why this is the case, we need to elaborate on part of our discussion from chapter 1. To do so, we will introduce the concept of "subculture."

SUBCULTURE AND CONTEXT

Subculture is a fairly easy concept to define and to observe, but its implications can be of significant consequence. Simply stated, a subculture is a culture that has formed within a host culture, sharing some of its assumptions but developing others (some of which are contradictory to the host) of its own. Subcultures exist across all layers of culture: mesocultures are subcultures to the macroculture; a town's microculture is a subculture to the regional and other mesocultures that flow through it; and a parish's microculture is a subculture of the community in which it is located. Furthermore, within any established organization, subcultures form around the different groups that emerge because of the organization's gradual differentiation of functions. In a congregation, some common subcultures include those that are associated with the choirs, the trustees, the deacons or elders, the paid staff, the church school department, women's societies, youth ministries, mission, and so on. In some churches, the subcultural lines also can run along familial ties: such-and-such a clan has wielded influence in one area, another clan in a different area, and so on. Similarly, a network of unrelated members can develop their own subcultural agendas.

SUBCULTURES IN CHURCHES

By the time a church develops subcultures, it has begun to negotiate the divergent claims that each one makes on the congregation. Choirs are interested in their schedule, music, robes, and special seasonal programs; trustees pay most of their attention to the church's budget, money, and property; mission groups want more church members to get involved with justice and social welfare needs; church school officials believe that learning is the key to a healthy, active congregation. Many pastors have experienced consternation on discovering that these various groups in the congregation sometimes behave as though they share no common purpose.

Churches at this stage of their life need a pastor who can navigate the sometimes deep waters among these various subcultures and who can help the congregation harmonize and align them within the wider scope of the church's vision.[13] Recognizing this need helps focus the new pastor's challenges, even though it points out how complicated those challenges might become. The logical question thus becomes, "Who is adopting me?" If the congregation consists of more than one group or network, with their own distinctive subcultures, how and with whom does the pastor's adoption occur?

SUBCULTURE AND POPULARITY

When I was serving as pastor of one particular church, I was asking a different kind of question. It became clear to me in the first several months that some members were not especially pleased to have me. Their reasons remained hidden, in spite of my efforts to make sense out of what seemed to be a premature, irrational attitude. So I proceeded by trying to answer the question, "How can I get the majority of members to approve of my ministry among them?" My assumption (in this case, implicit and assumed to be true for the congregation as well) was that "majority rules." If more than one-half of the congregation liked what I was doing, I reasoned, I was accepted and could continue developing programs.

As I came to realize only after leaving that congregation, my assumption—garnered from the democratic ideals of our American macroculture—was not widely held among the membership. I had figured out in the first six months that there were three men and one woman—all aged sixty and older and virtually lifelong members—whose opinions had more sway than the rest of the members. In my naïveté, however, I supposed that I could do an "end run" around their power by generating enough support from newer, younger members. What I witnessed instead was a "front-door, back-door" phenomenon. Younger people would get active in the congregation but then back away, once they ran into resistance by the "old guard." Just by the numbers, that church's membership, attendance, and participation had a chance to see an impressive net gain of twenty-five percent in only four years. Instead, by the time I had left in frustration for another call, membership, attendance, and giving were back to levels before my arrival.

One big mistake I made while pastor of that congregation was in failing to understand the power of a church's dominant subculture. The four members whom I had discerned as having such influence did not carry that influence as individuals. In a real sense, the culture of the congregation granted it to them. They were key culture-bearers in that church, and, in their eyes, they had something to protect. Since they perceived me as not trying to honor their culture, they were rightly suspicious of my actions and intentions. Yes, they wanted new members, but only as long as those new members also fit into the church's current way of life. I thought that I could change all that by ignoring what they revered. I was wrong, and I learned it the hard way. Not only this, but I left that congregation failing to have created conditions that would make it more likely that the church could begin to entertain change.

Was I adopted by this church? Well, all the newer and younger members accepted me as a capable and creative pastor. To them, I symbolized a future: young, eager, starting a family, open to new people and ideas. To all those who bore the dominant subculture of that congregation, however, my presence was viewed with caution. A small, modest church could not be too picky about pastors because it never attracted many candidates. This limitation, however, did not impede members of this church's dominant subculture from seeking to keep things as they had been. They were not convinced that I honored their way of being. I showed more indications of creating and supporting other and new subcultures instead. Subsequently, even though many members liked me, the congregation never really adopted me.

I wish that my experience was unusual among pastors but, unfortunately, it is all too common. Pastors often do not get adopted by their congregations. As a result, both pastor and parish feel a level of frustration about their partnership, about the meaning of ministry and mission, and, ultimately, about gospel-driven results. As I have said already, the point about adoption is not that it is based in popularity; rather, adoption is a metaphor that reveals the subtle dynamics involved in creating effective parish ministry. Pastors have to be assimilated into the culture, especially the dominant subculture, of their congregations. The degree to which that assimilation occurs circumscribes the degree of potential for the church's immediate future.

APPOINTMENT TRADITIONS AND ADOPTION

By this point in the chapter, readers who serve churches by appointment rather than a call might be wondering how much of this conversation applies to them. They might be asking whether it is possible for pastors who are appointed ever to be adopted by their congregations. On average, appointments have a shorter duration than calls. When I was in college, for instance, the pre-seminary students were told that appointments in United Methodist congregations averaged three years, while calls in (then) United Presbyterian congregations averaged six years. Having twice as much time to serve a congregation creates certain advantages. For one thing, it increases the likelihood that the pastor (stranger/guest) can enter the church's (host's) life effectively enough to be assimilated/adopted.

As we have defined it in this chapter, then, the notion of adoption, as it would operate in appointment systems, would be a modified form of what we can observe in churches who call their pastors. Parishes whose pastors are "charged" to them every year by the bishop do not have the same kind of control over who is appointed as churches who vote on the pastor's coming. This difference of the pastor's origin of arrival, linked with a different kind of certainty/uncertainty about the pastor's tenure, is a condition of the parish's life that gets internalized. Hence, it will shape some of the parish's underlying, shared assumptions.

Consider, for example, Methodist parishes (whether African Methodist Episcopal, African Methodist Episcopal Zion, Christian Methodist Episcopal, United Methodist, Wesleyan, Free Methodist, etc.) that have been small and modest in resources for virtually their entire existence. These are congregations who themselves know deep down that they do not have the cultural capital within their denomination to "bargain" with the bishop for a sophisticated, highly skilled, well-compensated pastor. In a decoding process, we would discover assumptions like these:

> "We will never amount to much."
> "Power is often out of our control: we have to take what the bishop gives us."
> "We don't get too close to our pastors, because even the best ones leave before we want them to."
> "We have to rely on ourselves, since we never know what we are going to get in our pastors."

While these kinds of shared assumptions are not necessarily upbeat, they nonetheless reveal important learnings that a congregation as described could possess.

Thus in congregations with appointed pastors, what it means to adopt their pastors very likely will have a different feel from that in churches with called pastors. Assimilation should have some different qualities to it. This awareness could cut both ways. It not only could explain a congregation's characteristic distance that it keeps from its pastor, but it could explain why a parish who has favorable experiences with their appointments might have developed a way to adopt the pastor more quickly. Such a "fast-track" adoption would depend, of course, on the pastor, who would not step on any of the larger land mines in that church's field of shared assumptions.

ADOPTION AND MARGINALITY

One thing that makes adoption somewhat tricky is that it never should turn into a total immersion. This point might seem contradictory and could certainly appear ironic. Yet, if a pastor is to maintain a capacity to lead the congregation, she or he must keep a certain cultural distance from it. Otherwise, the pastor very likely will not have the vantage point from which to discern the congregation's deep, underlying assumptions—those unconscious beliefs that drive the church. In Schein's words, "Leaders of mature organizations must . . . make themselves sufficiently marginal in their own organization to be able to perceive its assumptions objectively and nondefensively."[14]

This insight creates a counterpoint to the main theme of this chapter. It reminds us again that adoption is not about popularity per se, but about the pastor's being in a position to lead the congregation. Just as not getting adopted damages the pastor's ability to do ministry in the parish, so also does getting too "cozy" with it. Realistically, getting "overadopted" usually takes a number of years and incidents indicating that the pastor is not willing or able to help the congregation respond constructively to change. Yet the point is still worth making. We will see it spelled out further in the next chapter and again in chapter 5.

ADOPTION AS SURPRISE

One of the most unnerving experiences of a new pastorate can come from wondering if you have been assimilated, accepted, or adopted by the congregation. As was quoted from Gittins earlier in the chapter, the third stage of assimilation—incorporation—does not occur in some formal way that everyone would readily understand. In a way, it just happens; perhaps no one at first even realizes that it has taken place.

Janet was a second-career pastor, a mother whose children were grown and who had gone through a divorce before responding to the call to ministry. Following seminary graduation, she accepted a call to be pastor of a small, small-town church in a farming community. Janet was a bit disorganized, but her concern for people was easily evident. Her overall appearance and manner did not threaten the members of the congregation or the town; she was not an "executive" type, using this first parish as a stepping-stone to "bigger and better" things. Janet was content to be their pastor. After four years, however, she still felt in the dark: Was she having an impact on the church?

Some changes in Janet's family situation required her to move from her residence in town into more suitable lodgings. Inexplicably, certain members of the congregation strongly voiced their opposition to Janet's move. Some of them even were downright rude about it. Being sensitive, Janet was distressed. She began to second-guess her decision. Yet the time for making the move was approaching.

An incident occurred at the church in which one of the opponents to Janet's move expressed his opinion in the presence of Janet and other church members. After he left the room, Janet was attempting to recover from the shock of the verbal attack. Then one of the other members, an older man, said to Janet quietly, "We'll help you move." He organized a few families with pickups, and a small party descended on Janet's house. They moved furniture into the pickups, helped pack boxes, drove to the new house, moved everything into the new house, and helped Janet begin to arrange everything. She was very grateful for their help.

Janet recounted this story to me just weeks after it happened. As she told it, the pain and distress of the opposition to her move was apparent in her face and voice. This was an incident that still troubled her. So I asked her, "Were the ones who fought against your move newer members or long-time members?"

She thought for a moment. "Well, they haven't been members too many years."

"And who helped you to move?" I continued.

A certain recognition came to her face. "It was people who have been at the church a long time, the ones who run the church."

I smiled at her: "Then you have been adopted by the church. The members who moved you sound like the ones who bear the dominant subculture of the church. They were showing you that they have accepted you as their pastor."

Janet stood motionless as tears welled up in her eyes. She gazed aimlessly for a few moments and finally said, "I never realized that that was what was happening." Her face brightened, she smiled, and her body looked as though a weight had just been lifted off her back. We talked for a couple more minutes about how the adoption as their pastor had moved her into a new phase. She was now capable of deepening ministry with them.

This is the purpose of a pastor getting adopted by her or his church. What can happen next is the subject of chapter 3.

Making It Count

How Does "Busyness"
Turn into Ministry?

HAMMERS AND HEAVEN

A NUMBER OF YEARS AGO, a little article by a frustrated pastor appeared in *Monday Morning* magazine. *Monday Morning* is a periodical designed for pastors and other Presbyterians as a forum for issues and gripes that face the church in all its settings, challenges, and opportunities. When I served congregations, it seemed that the articles that got my attention tended to be those written by pastors struggling to be effective but somehow feeling thwarted along the way. This one particular article certainly filled the bill!

Its author, a pastor, told of a pastoral colleague who arrived home one afternoon in a foul mood. His wife noticed him entering the house, dropping everything he was carrying onto the kitchen table, and heading out to the garage, without so much as a "Hello" or "How was your day?" A few moments later, she could hear hammering, the nail-into-wood kind. He must have been starting a project at his workbench, she thought. Suddenly, her husband the pastor flung open the garage door to the house, striding in triumphantly, but looking fiercely determined. He was holding cupped in his outstretched arms, like an over-eager wise man in a bathrobe nativity play, a piece of 2 x 4 scrap, with a nail partially driven into it. "There!" he shouted to his wife and anyone on the block who could not have helped hearing him. "I did that!"

Continuing the article, the author wrote with earnest concern and wonderment about pastoral activity and ministry. "How many of us pastors feel as frustrated as my friend does?" he queried. What can a pastor do to reduce the amount of time spent on mundane chores and increase his or her impact on ministry? What has it come to in our congregations when the lay leadership seems more concerned about counting beans than in making ministry count?

This vivid image of the nail-driving pastor has stayed with me for a long time. When I first read it, I could easily identify with his frustration. I wanted my ministry to make a difference, to count for something, to strengthen the Christian witness of the congregation that I served, to address problems in its community. I left that particular church, and the next two as well, feeling that they were interested in something, but I was not always convinced that it was gospel ministry. Instead, it seemed to me that they all were preoccupied with details. I felt guilty about being so judgmental, but I saw no other way to understand the dynamics.

"GOD IS IN THE DETAILS"

In the years that have followed since, I have come to what I think is a more fully textured understanding of churches. This understanding has a lot to do with culture, and it has helped me to redirect my pastoral energy. I am less impatient with congregations and more willing to live with what seems to be the gap between where they are and where they could be. It is not a matter of capitulating to congregations that are halfhearted, misguided, barely inspired, or afraid: There are plenty of churches like this who need help! The difference for me now, though, is one of perspective. By being more realistic, I think pastors stand a better chance of getting their churches out of the bean-counting mode and fruitfully engaged in ministry in the name of Jesus the Christ.

The purpose of this chapter is to show how this can be done. Here we explore, using cultural capital as our key, how pastors can help congregations achieve ministry that is constructive. Once a pastor has settled in, has been assimilated and adopted by the church, she or he still will have many bean-counting demands placed on his or her time and energy. The opportunity in such a situation is in learning how to discern the cultural symbolism of the pastor's work. Here we will look at how to build pastoral strategy, taking this awareness of congregational culture into account. A pastor who is interpreting the symbolism of the church's life insightfully can better balance risky ventures with the congregation's particular readiness for new things. Such a pastor will come to appreciate how "God is in the details." Such a pastor will be able to generate within an imperfect community greater faith and witness.

JESUS WAS LUCKY

Part of the context creating the dynamic of busyness vs. ministry has to do with a particular aspect of our modern legacy. One of the significant occurrences during the twentieth century was the massive proliferation of human organizations. We who live in the United States organize everything! Businesses, schools, athletic associations (in schools, colleges, communities, minor and major professional leagues), hobby clubs, scholarly groups, business and professional associations, entertainment fan clubs, governmental bodies of all levels, "friends of the library/zoo/botanical garden" groups, neighborhood and homeowner associations, Internet chat groups—it seems as though nothing these days escapes being organized somehow.

With organization comes an inevitable amount of time spent on various necessary issues. Matters of clarifying the organization's purpose; agreeing on its activities; determining constituencies and membership requirements; allocating, utilizing, and accounting for resources; selecting structures, offices, and procedures and more, all demand attention and effort (these will be elaborated on later). There are times when all of us wish that we could return to a simpler time, with less complexity in our lives. Much of that complexity emerges because of our organized (but not necessarily more efficient) way of life.

Pastors sometimes wonder what went wrong between today and Jesus' time, when doing ministry seemed to be a lot less cluttered by meetings, phone calls, and e-mail. An examination of the gospels suggests to the active American a certain simplicity of structure to Jesus' ministry, an easier pace, with less distractions. Jesus was lucky! All he had to do was preach, teach, and heal. No one asked him to preside over meetings, file reports on time, adjust a budget in mid-year when revenue dropped, or add another youth choir. There it was: ministry in a pure mode! Is that too much to ask?

The kind of ministry that Jesus undertook, in its organizational form, was quite different from what most pastors face in today's settled congregations. Jesus was engaged in an itinerant ministry, one of traveling from place to place, speaking to hastily assembled groups, responding to spontaneous requests for dinner dates, treating ill persons, deciding on travel plans based on the current responses and reports from elsewhere, keeping a purse, and so on. Early on, he selected twelve men to share a special role in his mission. Their entourage grew and included women as well. Jesus was leading a movement, not pastoring First Church downtown.

MODELS OF PASTORAL ACTIVITY

Compare this form of ministry to a pastor's typical demands these days. There are deadlines to meet for printing bulletins and programs for regular weekly worship; persons sick and in the hospital to visit; classes for which to prepare; meetings to plan and attend; crises to respond to; facilities maintenance, renovation, or construction on which to check; staff members with whom to talk on programming, activities, and personnel matters; preaching to prepare; major projects of various kinds to be discussed with a number of different constituencies; preparation for the next fund-raiser; and so on. Then there is the unknown factor; as one of my colleagues once wryly put it, "Pastoral ministry is one long series of interruptions."

One way to put the matter of pastoral busyness vs. ministry in relief is by contrasting the stereotyped styles of suburban versus small-town churches.[1] In suburban settings, church members often are involved in secular pursuits that make a corporate model of running the congregation attractive. They strive for efficiency, set up structures, establish and follow procedures, try to make decisions based on reasonable factors and so on. Pastors are expected to be integrally involved in all of these processes.

In small-town and rural settings, however, this business-corporate model does not fit. Here, as we saw in the earlier summary of Sample's work, communities are based on long-standing relationships, clan-type ties. Setting goals is not as important as knowing what is going on with whom and being ready to help in times of need. Pastoral busyness in this context involves as much "hanging around" as making things happen.[2]

African American congregations have faced the tensions between the corporate and clan models—sometimes starkly. Once a primarily rural or small-town phenomenon, the African American church encountered many new challenges as it became established in urban areas following massive twentieth-century northern migrations. Former patterns of activity, as well as roles between pastor and congregation, were forced to adapt, often with resistance. The rural pastor's part-time, simpler duties were transformed into complex demands from the community, as well as the congregation.[3] Differences of pastoral expectations, rooted in these demographic shifts, are still points of contention today.

These two contrasting pastoral models, reflecting the sociocultural contexts of congregations that expect them, should not be taken lightly. The differences for their emergence and potential are essential for many pastors to appreciate. Yet, in spite of the notable distinctions of style between the two, the question still can be asked by the pastor: "How do I know that I am not just busy, but that I am doing ministry?" It is a valid question whether you spend much of your pastoral time in organized meetings or in informal church gatherings. This question has a particular salience for me, as I recall a comment made once by a woman seminarian. She was frustrated with pastors, she said, because whenever they got together, all they did was talk. None of them actually would do anything! Regardless of the overall accuracy of this observation, it is important for us to see how ministry emerges through the varied expectations and activity of a pastoral role.

CULTURAL CAPITAL AND MINISTRY

Ministry effectiveness can be addressed insightfully by framing it in the key terms of this book. Here we are using the notion of "cultural capital" to identify the source of a pastor's ability to do ministry. The "cultural" element of this notion reminds us that all of one's pastoral activity occurs in a specific context, one that has its own peculiar puzzles. For each church, the surrounding community and the congregation's way of life present before the pastor a rich, yet also somewhat enigmatic, world. It is a world possessed of its own inner logic, one that the pastor must decode. The "capital" element of this notion calls attention to an image of resources and assets that are recognized as worthy of exchange within that culture. As we saw in chapter 2, a pastor needs to develop enough cultural capital within the congregation to become assimilated into its cultural world.

Another way of making this point is to say that the pastor's activity symbolizes her or his assumptions about ministry. Any of those symbolic experiences either will add to, or detract from, the pastor's accumulation of cultural capital within the congregation in question. The wise pastor is one who begins to sense how that capital is accumulating, that is, what kinds of situations and activities are potent for accrual. Of course, the intent here is not to be cold and calculating, which probably would be detected and rejected by the congregation. Rather, as the pastor senses positive responses from the congregation about his or her activity, she or he learns the meaning of artifacts and begins to decipher some of the congregation's shared assumptions.

An old story illustrates this point in an obvious way. One of my seminary professors told of Pastor Handy, who went to a church in a typical old small town. He cared for the people and was well liked, but nothing dramatic or noteworthy marked his relationship with them. Then, one year, torrential rains visited the town, and, for the first time in decades, the river threatened to overflow its banks. Pastor Handy joined many men of the town, moving and setting up rows of sandbags along the riverbank. It was hard work and went on around the clock. Finally, the rains ended, the river crested, and the town was saved. When the crisis subsided, the hardworking pastor had become a hero in the eyes of the congregation. He was not a native, but he had helped them save their town. From then on, he was "their pastor." They would do just about anything Pastor Handy suggested because they knew that he cared about them and their livelihoods.

Perhaps unknowingly, Pastor Handy used a crisis to send his cultural capital through the roof. This point is instructive, for its obverse is also true: A pastor's failure to "come through" in a crisis can lead to a loss of cultural capital. A pastor who gives poor pastoral care through the death and funeral of a key church member, who embarrasses the congregation in public, who takes a stand on an issue contrary to the church risks damaging what cultural capital he or she has built up. As we have suggested in different ways already, it is thus incumbent on a pastor to learn the ways and meanings of the congregation.

MISSING AN OPPORTUNITY

One young pastor I know was thrown for quite a loop concerning the matter of flags in the sanctuary. A brief version of his experience is recounted in the macroculture section of chapter 1; here we examine it in terms of pastoral adoption. Rev. Case had served as pastor for several years of a congregation that had changed from an eight hundred-member, active place in the 1950s to a struggling group of barely one hundred by the 1980s. Their neighborhood had undergone two ethnic and religious transitions, but the desirability of the community had remained high in their urban area. A bit of the neighborhood's new diversity was reflected in the congregation and its activities, but the church was still getting smaller and older. Rev. Case had married and had a baby while serving this church, and he seemed well liked.

Then a fire in the church building required a lengthy cleanup and restoration process. A natural go-getter, Rev. Case oversaw many of the details. When it finally came time to replace smoke-damaged items from the sanctuary, the young, baby-boom pastor ascertained that this was a "teachable moment" for some applied theology. At a monthly official board meeting, he suggested that the American flag that had been on display in the sanctuary for years not be replaced, but that another Christian flag be purchased. After all, Rev. Case reminded them, we are Christians first, and we don't want the presence of both flags in the sanctuary to send a mixed message.

When Rev. Case brought up the episode with me a week later, he was still reeling from the response to his suggestion. This normally very self-confident pastor was unexpectedly stunned by the vociferous dissension that his "small" suggestion had generated among the congregation's elected officials. Not only did they tell him in no uncertain terms that they opposed his idea, but they also called their church friends right after the meeting, before they went to bed! For the first time in his limited years of pastoral ministry, Rev. Case realized that he could not insist on his way. He had stepped on a land mine in that congregation's field—a big one!

Rev. Case's experience illustrates the dangers of a pastor not learning—or worse, of ignoring, once deciphered—the congregation's basic shared assumptions. Too, the relationship between busyness and effective ministry looms large in this incident. Most of this church's remaining members had grown up during the Great Depression, World War II, and the Korean War. For them, the American flag is a symbol of the freedom, dearly paid for, that allows Americans to worship and live as they please. This is a shared assumption of their generation, part of American macroculture as they live it. Representing the dominant subculture of their congregation, these lay officials felt entitled and obligated to register their disagreement.

By contrast, Rev. Case grew up in an era that questioned authority, government, and war. For him and many of his generation, the American flag is a mixed symbol, tainted by the civil rights struggle and the Vietnam War. This baby-boomer, mesocultural, shared assumption historically has been viewed at odds with the flag assumption from the earlier generation. Even though these two assumptions originate from outside the congregation, Rev. Case's request triggered the tension between them.

In other contexts, this incident could have cost Rev. Case his job. He could have lost so much of his cultural capital with the congregation that they could not trust or respect him anymore. However, he had served them satisfactorily long enough that he survived the storm—with a couple of well-placed apologies to war-veteran members. It was through his management of some of the church's busyness that Rev. Case was reminded, quite abruptly, that ministry, or the lack of it, can occur in just about any set of circumstances.

LEARNING THE CONGREGATION'S SHARED ASSUMPTIONS

Rev. Case's story helps us articulate a couple of valuable questions. These are queries to ourselves as pastors, ways to help us reframe the matter of whether our daily activity is relevant to ministry or not. One of these questions is: "Have you discovered which of the church's shared assumptions are supported by which of its artifacts?"

When we first enter a congregation, we are going to be busy doing things and learning the lay of the land. As time goes by, however, we will become familiar with some of the congregation's artifacts. It also will become apparent to us that these artifacts have particular meanings to the congregation. Some of that meaning will be articulated, as an espoused value. Yet, if there is one thing that pastors need to learn about their churches, it is that what they say is not all of what you get. In other words, something deeper is also at stake, only partially expressed by the spoken meaning (espoused value). That deeper stream taps into the congregation's shared, basic assumptions. Pastors become effective first as they discover what these assumptions are.

The second question for interpreting pastoral busyness that moves the pastor from detective work to personal reflection is: "Are your own espoused values for Christian faith and life compatible with those of the congregation?"

This question must be approached in different ways, depending on how you began your ministry with your current church. If you founded the congregation, your espoused values are being tested along the way by the members, to see if they actually do help them become a healthy church. If you have arrived at the congregation through a call process, you and the search committee will have exchanged a number of statements that reveal some of your and their espoused values. This exchange helped both of you decide that the match between the two of you held promise for mutually beneficial ministry. If you were appointed to the church, you have had to listen carefully right away, in order to begin identifying the congregation's values.

Regardless of how you became the pastor, one way to understand your major challenge to authentic ministry with the congregation is through this question about matching espoused values. What you say is important to you as a pastor needs to bear some significant relationship to what the church says is important. However, we already have seen that the culture of the congregation goes deeper than words. The purpose of paying attention to espoused values is so that you as pastor have a reference point for assessing your impact. Espoused values link artifacts with assumptions, in various ways. Sometimes the link is fairly direct; in certain other cases, the link might be contradictory. Either way, there is something important for the pastor to figure out. You cannot help the congregation stretch its vision and ministry until you first honor its culture. All along the way, this two-step challenge will draw your pastoral attention to all three levels of culture.

EXAMPLES OF UNCOVERING ASSUMPTIONS

In chapter 1, we looked at a list of basic, shared assumptions that could be part of the culture of a church that you have served. Let us here look in a little more detail at some of those kinds of assumptions that you might decipher in the congregation that you serve. Being able to "play to" certain of these assumptions helps you as pastor establish yourself as being "on their side." This is a necessary position to gain—a level of cultural capital. Yet, we should be clear that not all of the congregation's shared assumptions necessarily will be helpful ones—to them or to any potential that you might see for their ministry. Learning how to navigate the waters between such assumptions is one of the skills of a pastor's cultural wisdom.

Take, for instance, this generic version of a shared assumption of which I have become aware in several well-established congregations over the years: *Having important power in this church is possible only for a few who have been here for a long time.*

For a newcomer to the church, whether a member, staff person, or the pastor, uncovering this assumption might appear to be revealing dirty laundry. It might seem wrong or un-Christian for a congregation to believe, deep down, that not everyone has an equal influence. Theologically, there might be a normative case that could be made against this kind of shared assumption. Realistically and culturally, however, this assumption needs only to function as a description of the way things are. It would be silly for newcomers to expect that they would be received, tested, trusted, and granted positions of influence quickly. Churches, like other organizations, need to develop stability and some predictable patterns and understandings to create a culture that can support a healthy church.

Earlier in its life, this assumption about power might have helped the church stay a course and achieve some positive results. In later years, though, the same assumption can prevent important contributions from people who can help the congregation gain fresh vitality. Yet, if the pastor tries to tackle such an assumption head-on, the key culture-bearers in the church might resist strenuously. As a pastor in such a situation, you will stand a better chance of increasing your cultural capital by finding ways to bring deserved recognition to the persons and values that are represented by the assumption. From there, you are in a stronger position to espouse and model an eventual modification of this assumption.

Another assumption that I have encountered is: *Embarrassing secrets should stay that way*.

In some congregations, it is not considered part of their community practice to discuss in public any troubles that the church has had. There could be a number of different explanations in the congregation's history for why this assumption was learned: All the members are related to each other; the church views itself as the most prominent one in the community and wants to preserve its perceived reputation; the ethnic culture of the people who founded the church values privacy; and so on. We saw in chapter 2 how the Rev. Jones lost his pastorate at St. James Church in the wake of the congregation's reaction to his causing their trusted treasurer to be arrested. An assumption of this kind seems to have been a strong one in St. James's culture.

Perhaps one of the most commonly shared assumptions in churches goes something like this: *Our church will never be special, but we try to be good*.

We live in a macroculture that values size, dramatic display, and noticeable achievement. Contrast these values with the fact that the majority of local churches have memberships of two hundred or less. Since many of these congregations are established and experience little change in membership, they come to accept their modest status. Their sense of accomplishment centers on familiar customs, practices, and relationships—especially since many of them exist in oral cultures. Pastors who serve churches with this assumption can help them strengthen their ministry by identifying and honoring the place of artifacts that uphold expressions of this assumption in positive forms.

One more shared assumption seems fairly widespread among churches, and, as assumptions often do, this one cuts two ways: *We expect our pastor to take care of things, as long as it fits with our way of life.*

Many congregations come to view the pastoral role in a comprehensive way. That is, they want the pastor to attend to many of the regular details of operation, along with the more "ministerial" expectations of worship, preaching, teaching, calling, crisis care, and so forth. At times, I have thought of this view of the pastor's role as one of being the congregation's "professional Christian"! Some pastors might accept this assumption without question and work strenuously to fulfill it. Others might try to resist it openly. Again, pastors who find out—even unexpectedly—one of the church's assumptions will not be successful if they try to change it right away. Attending to the details, while keeping an eye out for the right opportunity to expand the church's view of its life and ministry, is the wiser and more effective course of action.

BUSYNESS, VISION, AND MINISTRY

In this chapter, we have been looking at aspects of congregational culture, with an eye toward how a pastor develops cultural capital. Our specific aim has been to see how pastors can find their way, from the standpoint of daily pastoral activity, beyond a preoccupation with routines. Being busy does not necessarily mean that the pastor is engaged in ministry, but neither does busyness automatically negate the chance for ministry. Pastors who recognize this tension are more likely better equipped to live in it creatively. Not only this, but pastors who have been doing their cultural homework stand a better chance to see the particular ministry opportunities that are available, as well as already have the cultural resources for capitalizing on them.

Before we venture on to another theme in the next chapter, let us look at the present theme of busy-ness and ministry using one more vantage point. I am thinking in particular about vision and the key place that vision needs to have in a church and in the heart of a pastor's work. Vision is a topic that has received much deserved attention over the last several years.[4] Yet, as with many important notions, vision also can be misunderstood and even cheapened by an inadequate definition. In brief, vision for a church is that distinctive picture of a possible future to which the congregation senses God calling it. Vision is less about buildings or other resources and more about what buildings and resources can accomplish for the gospel. Every attractive vision also has a singular quality to it—something that grounds it in the specific context and opportunities of the given congregation. A vision that is clear, articulated, and compelling is one that a congregation can see itself following.[5] Excitement, motivation, and commitment all ensue when a church sets its sights on the horizon of a worthwhile vision.

The hope is that the reader already begins to see some of the implications of this view of vision for the work of the pastor. *Pastors do ministry when they help their congregations keep a vision before them in all that they do.* In the terms of this book, vision consists of a particular set of espoused values, some of which are already being enacted, some of which are comfortable and a few that are new in some way. The pastor's challenge is to help the congregation put this set of values to the test, so to speak. In order to create new assumptions, or discover along the way which old assumptions need altering, the congregation applies the values named by the vision to all the decisions that they make.

These decisions can be classified in three distinct but necessary categories, ones that every organization and every local church must take into account.[6] In simple terms, these categories are:

- *What*—the church's programs and activities (worship, prayer meetings, revivals, church school and other educational events, choirs and music, dinners, seasonal events, work trips, soup kitchens, etc.)

- *Who*—the church's constituencies, both actual and potential (members, regular non-member attendees, visitors, non-active family of members, staff, nearby residents and business owners, government agencies that regulate activities and use of property, etc.)
- *How*—the processes and structures, whether formal or informal, used to make the church's resources (pastoral and other staff positions, denominational disciplines and laws, constitution, organizational structure, actual procedures in use, etc.) available to serve its activities and people

These three categories are functions of every church. Taken together with vision (the why, or purpose, function), the four functions infuse the demands on a pastor's time. That is, whether a pastor likes it or not, there is no way for a church to avoid decisions that address its purpose, program, people, and processes. One pastoral temptation is to favor one of the functions over the others, for example, programming. If a pastor loves to cook up ideas for the church to do (what), but neglects developing congregational camaraderie (who), eventually neither programming nor people needs will be effectively met. Likewise, if the pastor loves to spend time with church members but does not help church organizations operate smoothly and with unified purpose, the church's ministry will suffer.

A pastor can get busy, even too busy, attending to one or two of the basic functions at the expense of the others. Regardless of his or her personal preference or style, a pastor engaged in ministry for the sake of the congregation attends to all four functions—what, who, how, and why. A pastor who is helping the congregation affirm its distinctive ministry and mission is one who has developed cultural capital in all areas. More precisely, the pastor gets "invested" in the church's programs, people, and processes, in order to win its understanding and trust (see chapter 2). The cultural capital developed here then makes it possible for the pastor to help the congregation look at the long-term, its purpose and vision.

RECOVERING FOR A REASON

Rev. Bruce was appointed pastor of a small, thirty-five-year-old church in a small Southern town. As is the case with many African American congregations, the church met just twice a month because their financial resources could not support a pastor full time. A tall man with a warm smile and passion for parish ministry, Rev. Bruce discovered early on that the parish had undergone a fight and split just a few years before. In the faces and behavior of the members, he could see that they were still hurting. Yet, he could not get close to them for they had become suspicious of pastors— the split had been precipitated by one of its recent clergy.

In his first few years with this congregation, Rev. Bruce found himself preaching often on themes of forgiveness and grace. He wanted them to feel good about themselves again. He made himself available to members in a nonjudgmental, supportive way. He drove to their town during the week in order to attend all of their special events. For a long time, this caring pastor wondered if he was getting anywhere with this reticent, paralyzed community of faith. Gradually, however, members began to open up to him, sharing about the pain of the conflict and their hopes in faith. Each year, the bishop saw fit to reappoint him to the same parish. In the fifth year, Rev. Bruce noticed that members began asking if they could try some new activities. He gave them his unqualified support. Participation in church activities began to increase, the finances got stronger, and the congregation was feeling better about itself. Rev. Bruce then began watching for opportunities to help the congregation talk together about their future, about a fresh vision of their possibilities with God.

When does busyness turn into ministry? In Rev. Bruce's case, it was when the slow busyness of "being present with" a crippled community eventually persuaded the people that he was there for their benefit. Rev. Bruce's experience offers no quick formula for the rest of us, because the needs of any given congregation can vary so much. Yet we can generalize in one way: His behavior symbolized an honoring of their values and assumptions, eventually creating enough cultural capital for him to help them move ahead. There is no way to predict just how such a process of pastoral involvement will yield its results. Instead, if we pastors will honor the richness of what we encounter, the congregation will come to see us as its ally. We can move past the adoption, past the feeling of just being busy, and into a mutual enlistment of gospel-driven ministry.

The pastor who has reached this point of getting along with her or his church is in a stronger position to help it deal with tough issues. To this delicate, but hardly unavoidable, topic we now turn.

Effective Delivery

Who Can Carry Bad News?

AN UNEXPECTED JOLT

IT WAS NOT A MEETING to which the bishop had been looking forward. For several years, the diocese had provided the struggling parish with funds to augment its meager budget. But things were not improving: St. Agnes Church seemed to be getting swallowed up by all the new things in its neighborhood. Homeless people looking for food and a warm place to sleep traveled the same sidewalks as the young, urban professionals who hustled early each morning to a fast-paced job in one of the skyscrapers downtown. Crime was up, but so were property values. Few of St. Agnes's remaining three score members lived close by anymore, so the diocesan parish aid committee had met with the bishop and decided that it was time to pull the plug.

Vestry members greeted the bishop cordially, but with tired resignation, after he parked on a narrow street and walked a block to an ample stone structure, whose glory days could still be glimpsed here and there in its noble skyline visage. With the greetings and other introductory business out of the way, the bishop spoke. "You know that I am here to close your church. But first, tell me: What has it been like to be in this parish?"

One by one, the vestry members, mostly retired, recounted stories of St. Agnes Church. Woven unevenly in with tales of trying to keep the building maintained were flashbacks of times not that long ago, vivid images from their youthful years when the parish thrived. Without rancor or accusation, these long-faithful members of St. Agnes Church painted on a canvas a fading picture of their church, once active and confident, but now overwhelmed by the stench of urine on its back steps and the arthritis afflicting most of its members.

For almost an hour, the bishop listened. The stories seemed to get heavier and heavier. Finally, as if there was nothing more to say, the room became quiet, the words of their recitations practically hanging in the air like dark gray fog. At one corner of the table, a white-haired woman in her eighties named Esther had been sitting quietly. Suddenly, in the midst of their moment of heavy silence, Esther sat up in her chair, leaned toward the bishop and said, "Bishop, we're dead, aren't we? We're dead!"

Her colleagues sat up so quickly that one might have thought that a jolt of electricity had just passed around the table through each one! A few of them blinked their eyes, the way that someone does when they have just awakened from a deep sleep. Others turned their heads this way and that, staring at the faces of church companions they had known for so many years. The bishop waited to see what would happen next.

No one got angry. No one stood up in a huff and walked out of the room. No one accused the elderly woman of betraying her dear congregation. Instead, slowly, they began to speak again. This time, though, something was different. The stories that they first had told the bishop were stories that everyone there already knew. But of what would this next conversation consist? What would these long-standing, committed officials of their parish say, now that one of their own had just called their church "dead"? No one knew for sure. So they talked again, and, this time, everyone was listening very closely.

DELIVERING BAD NEWS

This dramatic moment in the life of St. Agnes Church could be approached and discussed from many angles. We could note the bishop's skillful pastoral care of a disheartened cadre of parish leaders. We could inquire about the members' theological and spiritual condition at the time. We could speculate on how well they understood the changes that were occurring in the neighborhood of their church facilities. But the perspective that bears the most on our exploration of cultural capital for ministry has to do with bad news. In particular, how can a congregation deal with situations or issues that threaten discord? How does a pastor play a role that stands some chance of being helpful rather than upsetting?

The answer to these critical questions is revealed in the story of St. Agnes's. It is an answer that many pastors seem never to understand, and, thus, the churches that they serve suffer because of it. Notice who in the story above delivered the bad news, who named the truth about the church in a way that was painful but still needed to be heard. It was not the bishop, though he might have been tempted to say something like, "The diocese has decided to close your parish, because it is dead now and has no future." How might the vestry members have responded to such a statement?

To his credit, the bishop made no such comment. Instead, he allowed the members of the vestry, the elected official board of the parish, to tell the story in their own way, to lay out their picture of what their church had been and was now. It was through this process that someone who "had the right" to deliver the bad news spoke up. She had been a member of that congregation for at least forty years. She was a person of faith and faithful to her church, having held virtually every post in the parish that was available to her. Every other vestry member trusted her and knew that whatever she did or said was with the utmost of integrity.

"Bishop, we're dead, aren't we? We're dead!" This searing pronouncement of the bare truth about St. Agnes Church came from Esther, one of the key culture-bearers of the congregation. No question about it, this was bad news! No one wanted to hear it, just as none of us do when the truth that we must face hurts. Yet, the fact that Esther named the truth about St. Agnes Church opened the door for the other culture-bearing members of that struggling congregation to face reality together. As a result of their newly claimed honesty, the vestry of St. Agnes Church was able to make some important decisions that it might otherwise never have reached on its own (we will found out later in the chapter what happened!).

PASTORS AND BAD NEWS

This chapter tackles one of the touchier subjects of pastoral ministry— namely, the matter of who in a congregation can tell it what it needs to hear when that news is not what anyone wants to hear. Closely linked to this question of appropriate messengers is that of fitting means: How can the message be delivered in such a way so that it has the greatest chance of helping the church? Pastors need to realize that they often are not the ones to do it. It will be the purpose of this chapter to help pastors learn how to discern the people who can bring the bad news. This issue is so crucial: Churches in the foreseeable future, if they are to stay strong in gospel witness, will continue to meet challenges that must be faced well.

The question of dealing with bad news in local churches has a particular relevance, because of the historic impact and legacy of the 1960s. During that era, so many topics with far-reaching consequences erupted into the American public arena. Civil rights, military involvement in Southeast Asia, the sexual revolution, women's equality, and other issues pressed for attention, aided by the unprecedented effect of television coverage. During this period, it was easy to find discussions in many religious quarters promoting the role of the pastor as prophet. Modeled after figures in the Hebrew Scriptures, modern-day prophets were encouraged to stand up, speak out in church and community about evil and injustice, and let the chips fall where they may. The assumption seemed to be that there are times when it is most important just to speak a word from God.

From a practical standpoint, much of the prophetic ministry by those courageous pastors in the 1960s fell on deaf ears. Many congregations went right on with their business as usual, as though nothing needed attention or change. Some resisted dealing with what the prophet-pastors had to say. Not infrequently, churches told these pastors to leave. By the middle 1970s, when United States involvement in Vietnam ended and the equal rights amendment was defeated, the effects of prophetic preaching and activity on local churches were minimal. This was particularly the case among mainstream Protestant denominations that are mostly white, middle-class, and not too inclined to take social or political positions at odds with the status quo.

BEING RIGHT, OR BEING EFFECTIVE?

As an assessment of prophetic ministry, this quick look back at the turbulent 1960s should not be viewed merely as criticism. My point is not that prophetic ministry is wrong, for we cannot explain away its biblical presence and impact. However, from the perspective of ministry in a local church, I am suggesting that there are some things that pastors can learn in retrospect. If our primary purpose is to try to prove a point about what is socially or ethically right, being prophetic has its place. Yet, if our primary purpose is to help a congregation wrestle with important issues and come through the struggle with a new name and identity (as Jacob did with God's messenger in Gen. 32:22–32), our pastoral strategy will be different.

Jesus' own earthly activity reveals the sometimes complex relationships that can emerge between various forms of ministry. Whether an audience received good news or bad news from Jesus depended on his perception of their willingness to follow God's purposes. In Mark, Jesus teaches (1:21–28), heals (1:29–34), preaches (1:38–39), and attracts many "crowds" as a result (see 2:2; 3:20; 4:1; and 5:21). These large, transient groups seem to have consisted of people from the particular locale who were curious about what they had heard of Jesus and wanted to witness his ministry in action. Those who traveled with Jesus were his "disciples," a group much smaller in size than crowds, made up of those who felt led to give virtually all of their time to supporting Jesus' ministry (see Mark 2:18; 3:7–9; 4:33–34). "The twelve," all men, were specially selected for preaching and healing missions (3:13–19).

In his dealings with these several constituencies—and in all likelihood mostly peasants—Jesus brought a ministry of repentance, wholeness, and hope. For the religious leadership among Jesus' people, however, Jesus' activity often was seen as a threat. Indeed, Jesus is portrayed in Mark as challenging the emphases of the scribes and Pharisees (Mark 7:1-13). He thwarts their efforts to catch him in some misinterpretation of religious law (see Mark 10:2-9) or in blasphemy (Mark 11:27-33 on his authority). His skill in keeping these powerful compatriots off-guard made him very unpopular with them early in his ministry, to the point of wanting him done away with (3:6; 14:1-2).

It would be difficult, therefore, to use Jesus as a model for the same kind of almost adversarial prophetic role that we see in an Amos or Jeremiah. In a sense, we could say that Jesus' ministry was more well-rounded. He had his community, the crowds, the inner circle, and some weighty adversaries. Even Matthew's (chapter 23) and Luke's (11:37–54) stronger critique by Jesus of the scribes and Pharisees does not shift the balance away from healing, teaching, and preaching. Yes, Jesus delivered bad news here and there, but he did other important things, too. In recognizing his role as Messiah, we have to concede theologically that it is not a pastor's job to take Jesus' place! Being prophetic in a church is one kind of delivering bad news. From the perspective that we are developing in this book, we do not intend to eliminate the need for prophetic voices in and for local congregations. In our zeal, however, sometimes we pastors might not be very wise about strategy and tactics. Effective delivery of bad news depends a lot on who is the messenger and on how the delivery is made. I am claiming that our wisdom about such matters can be enhanced by understanding the impact of cultural capital within the congregation.

So, who has the cultural capital in a given church to bear bad news, let alone pay attention to it? That depends on some elements of culture that we discussed in earlier chapters and will elaborate further here.

THE "EVOLUTION" OF YOUR CONGREGATION'S CULTURE

When we look at our congregations through the lens of culture, we begin to see some things that might not have appeared as evident otherwise. In chapter 1, for instance, we discussed culture's three levels. Artifacts of culture include everything that we can observe about a community's objects, relationships, and behaviors. Church artifacts normally include items such as worship rituals and articles, facilities and their use, crosses, and so much more. In themselves, though, artifacts are not self-explanatory; their meaning extends into the other two levels of culture. Espoused values are those ideas of importance that members of the culture can and do declare. "This is a warm and friendly church," "We are committed to mission," and "Children are the future of the church" are all examples of espoused values. They are significant in a church's culture because of the ways in which they reflect what the congregation says it aspires to be and do.

Spoken values, along with artifacts, do not contain a church's culture, however. Its third level, shared basic assumptions, is the deepest and most important. These assumptions in many respects are practically hidden, since they are taken for granted by longtime church members. Unless something happens in the congregation's life that is perceived to challenge one of them, assumptions remain somewhat subterranean. Yet they are the most important level of culture, for assumptions develop into a pattern that guides the church's life, in both obvious and subtle ways.

News that is potentially bad links one of the church's deep assumptions with current data or a proposed practice that would undermine that assumption's continued validity. For instance, a well-established church can end up being situated in a neighborhood that no longer consists of people like those who first populated the church. Newcomers to the congregation might point out what to them appears to be this obvious fact for concern, only to hear a longtime member reply, "Oh, we'll be fine; we have overcome much worse situations than this." The shared assumption, having to do with the church's innate ability to survive any appearance of adverse circumstances, was created in earlier years because it was true for the church at some point in time. Since, however, the context giving rise to that assumption has changed, the assumption itself might not be true anymore.

Hence, attempting to bring to this church's attention any information or opinion that would call this assumption of survivability into question is an act of delivering bad news. If a pastor has not been adopted by the congregation, she or he should not try to bring such bad news, at least not by himself or herself. The actual cultural capital in the new-pastor scenario dwells elsewhere in the congregation, mostly likely among a handful of longtime members whom we could call (along with Esther of St. Agnes Church) the key culture-bearers. These culture-bearers know the lay of the church's cultural land; even though they might not be able to say so, they know where the land mines are. Since they are so heavily invested in that culture, they have the capital to risk triggering an explosion. This is why Esther "got away with" telling the bishop, in front of her fellow parishioners, that their parish was dead.

Therefore, when a well-established church needs to deal with bad news, it is the pastor's strategic role to create conditions within which one of the key culture-bearers will name the truth about the church in that situation. In order to make this possible, the pastor first will have to have become adopted and begun accumulating some cultural capital within the congregation. This strategy underscores the importance of the adoption/assimilation process that we discussed in chapter 2. New pastors should not be in a hurry to tell their congregations what is "wrong" with them and what they "need to do!" As part of their adoption experience, new pastors should be learning, and appreciating, the cultural network that operates in their church.

UNDERSTANDING THE "MODIFICATIONS"

This cultural strategy for bad news will be effective in many, if not most, congregations in existence today. That is because the vast majority of these congregations have been around for a number of years; they have created their many artifacts, articulated many espoused values and tested those values to create their shared basic assumptions. Yet, this strategy is not a universal one because a congregation's culture changes over its lifetime. Thus, we need to understand something about the basic nature of these culture changes. From here, we then will have identified three distinct strategies for bad news. And we will understand why, as pastors, we will not have the luxury of choosing which one best suits our church.

THE UP-AND-COMING CHURCH[1]

Congregations that are new or within about twenty-five years of age tend still to be creating their life and culture. As we just said, culture forms in an organization when the new group tests out the leader's values in its day-to-day operations and finds them to work. The configuration of assumptions that develops from this testing becomes shared among the members and defines its culture. Yet, in the parish's early years, this configuration is still taking shape; many aspects of the culture are, in a sense, up for grabs. In a young congregation, those key persons whose values are set forth and put to the test contribute to the process of helping create culture.

In some churches, this role might be played out primarily by the founding pastor. In church traditions with local autonomy, churches are often begun with one person at the center—the founding pastor. She or he articulates the vision of this new community of faith. Other persons gather around him or her, as they are persuaded by the vision's attractiveness. Because the founding pastor invests so many personal resources into the new church, his or her word and will become central. Members find out, through their own experiences with the fledgling congregation, whether the pastor can be trusted. Will this new vision come to be? With a founding pastor on the scene, the culture emerges from her or his leadership, whatever it is. Hence, if there is bad news to face, the pastor or a trusted colleague of the pastor is in the best cultural position to deliver it.

In other congregations, this function ends up getting lodged within a network of members. Perhaps they all were charter members; perhaps they are all related to each other, as a family or clan; perhaps they saw the opportunity and seized it. This form of culture creation frequently occurs in appointment systems, where the pastor often does not stay long enough at the beginning to be viewed as a cultural shaper. The newly appointed pastor in a church that is still defining its culture must negotiate his or her role amidst the (sometimes subtle) interests and activities of this member network. If the prospect seems a bit daunting, it certainly can be complicated!

THE ESTABLISHED CHURCH[2]

Once a congregation has existed for a number of years and gains an institutionalized feel to it, its culture (at least the one at this point in its life) has taken on contours that are comfortable to the longer-time members. These persons intuitively know who among them are the pivotal, key bearers of their church's culture. A church in this phase of its life is relatively healthy because it has survived various challenges and formed assumptions based on what has seemed so far to be effective. At this point, too, there have emerged subcultures within the congregation. These subcultures often grow out of the church's several program emphases—worship, music, education, fellowship, youth, finances/property, and so on. Many of the common skirmishes that transpire in an established congregation derive from differing interests among these subcultures.

Established congregations thus have a potentially more complicated relationship to bad news. The shared assumption(s) that could be threatened by such news might be more important to one subculture than to another. Troubling developments concerning finances, property, staffing, worship features, education, or other programs will be valued a little differently among the church's many organizations. The pastor is faced with figuring out which constituencies in the congregation will be distressed, which ones will be concerned, which ones might be apathetic or even pleased. As one might guess, this is not a simple task, especially if the pastor has not yet learned much about the congregation's culture.

Such potential confusion to the pastor, however, does not eliminate or reduce the need to become culture-smart. Which key culture-bearer has the cultural capital to help the church see what it needs to see? Creating the conditions within which this person will become evident is one of the challenges. Creating the conditions within which this person will speak the truth in love is the crux of the challenge.

THE WEAKENING CHURCH[3]

Congregations that have lost some of their vitality and flexibility often gradually weaken. They become more rigid about the way things are done. Both energy and activity begin to wane. They seek to preserve artifacts of a bygone era, during which their earlier strength grew out of success in meeting the challenges of the day. Privately, longtime church members fear for the future, as they intuitively realize that their shared assumptions are not serving them effectively any longer. It is in this phase of its life that the distinctions between the church's espoused values and its basic assumptions widen into rifts and then chasms.

Pastors of weakening churches have the greatest challenge in how to treat bad news. If the pastor has been too fully enculturated, she or he will be just as unlikely as anyone else even to recognize a problem, let alone face it. If, however, the pastor has maintained some objectivity within the congregation, any hard issues that appear on the horizon will register on his or her radar. Then the task of creating conditions for key culture-bearers to name the truth lay at hand. These persons, who are understood within the dominant subculture to have a high investment in the church, are best equipped with cultural capital. Helping them name the hard issue privately, in a safe setting, is a significant first step in its reception by the congregation.

A NEW LEASE ON LIFE

The bishop who visited St. Agnes Church knew that it was a weakened parish. As we saw, however, his tactic was to listen to the church's officers, to see if the truth would be named. Esther was the one who did so, as a key culture-bearer, and her action proved to be redemptive. By the end of their conversation with the bishop that evening, the vestry of St. Agnes decided that they wanted another crack at ministry. New ideas for outreach were shared. Fresh energy appeared on the vestry members' faces. Convinced that they could benefit from another chance, the bishop agreed to keep St. Agnes open. Four years later, the parish was fully self-supporting again.

In itself, bad news should not be avoided. Our biblical ancestors testify time and again to the redemptive power of owning up to the way things are, whether we like them or not, whether we are proud of them or not. As Paul says, "while we still were sinners Christ died for us" (Rom. 5:8). Indeed, perhaps some of our congregation's most profound experiences will depend first on receiving bad news. With wisdom, pastors can help these kinds of transformational opportunities occur.

THE WORD FROM MAUDE

Maude had been a member of her well-established congregation since young adulthood. One of the more prestigious churches in its town, Maude's church was proud of its prominent stone sanctuary and location. Maude raised her family in this church and, over the decades, was elected to every position available to her. In her eighties, Maude walked with a cane but was still known as a person of faith and conviction.

Late every calendar year, Maude's church held a potluck meal as the officers presented the budget for the following year. Everyone had copies of the proposals and could ask questions of the budget committee. One year as usual, the potluck was held and the proposed budget distributed. A couple of the committee members made the usual presentation about why this and that item was changing. The time for questions from the floor arrived. In the large hall, Maude stood up from her chair and walked haltingly with her cane to the microphone. She began to speak.

"I think the church should be ashamed that it gives so little money to mission!" she said. "Why, in the past, we have given a much higher percentage, even when times were hard." She went on with a few illustrations and an appeal to Christian generosity. She ended her speech by stating, "I move that the church board make sure that our mission-giving dollars stay at ten percent of our annual operating budget."

Maude hobbled back to her chair. The room was very still for a moment before someone seconded the motion. The budget committee chairperson asked for any discussion; there was none. The motion passed unanimously, and Maude's church kept to its ten percent mission formula for many years.

It takes a Maude to deliver the truth about hard issues in a potent way. It takes a pastor who knows how to get along with his or her church to activate the wisdom for handling the church's bad news redemptively.

Ahead of the Troops

How Do Pastors Become Leaders?

PORTRAIT OF ACHIEVEMENT

B Y MOST ACCOUNTS, Rev. Ms. Blake would not have been picked out of a pastor's lineup as the one who had turned a church around. Middle-aged, quiet and unassuming, married, employed in a professional management position, Rev. Blake had responded to God's call in her life. Persuaded of her fitness for pastoral ministry, her denomination commenced the process toward her eventual full ministerial membership. Part of that process included an assignment by the bishop to a part-time position in the smallest congregation of the district—twelve members.

When she arrived, Rev. Blake found this rural congregation low in morale, resentful toward being the "dumping ground" for pastors who were being punished, and bereft of spiritual energy. Ringing in her ears was the statement made to her by one of her colleagues who knew this tiny church's reputation: "Nothing good will ever come out of that church." Shocked and troubled by this commonly held outlook on her new charge, Rev. Blake prayed that she could do something about it.

Four years later, at the annual district convention, Rev. Blake and the church's delegates truly had cause to celebrate. Their church now boasted one hundred members, most of them active weekly. The church's annual budget had skyrocketed in that time, from a paltry $2,500 to over $65,000. Denominational apportionments were paid in full and on time; improvements were being made to the church building; teenagers were active in Bible study and prayer; countywide events were being cohosted by the congregation; and the members were feeling good about their future. They had a strong sense of spiritual support and direction; they began to reach out to their neighbors and friends with new energy. Perhaps most moving to Rev. Blake, the members expressed their appreciation and respect for her regularly. She was their pastor! So convinced they were that she was good for their church that they wrote the bishop requesting that he allow her to stay longer than the usual brief terms of her predecessors.

Certainly at the heart of this dramatic turn of events in this small, "insignificant" congregation was its new pastor. A deeply devoted and modest person, Rev. Blake is not the kind of pastor who seeks glory. I believe that this is one of several factors that worked together to make her ministry in this forgotten congregation so potent. However, piety and humility alone do not a leader make. Intuitively, Rev. Blake did some things right! Because of this, her church will never be the same.

LEADERSHIP: A SLIPPERY EEL

It is critical for pastors to learn the kinds of practical wisdom that help the Rev. Blakes among our churches to lead them well. Leadership has not been the sole topic of this book because of my concern that it might be treated without regard for the intricacies that entangle it. When Jesus said, "Whoever wants to be first must be last of all and servant of all" (Mark 9:35), he spoke a word that cuts to the heart of pastoral motivation and integrity. Getting along with your church does not mean never leading it. Neither does leadership mean drawing attention to yourself as the pastor. Leadership is not as easy or proverbial as it might first appear, and it certainly does not require a dominating personality.

Yet there is even more that needs to be said about pastoral leadership, since the notion of leadership is often misunderstood. In this chapter, we will seek to clarify the constitution of leadership in the context of a cultural understanding of the pastoral role. We will highlight our current, particular historical setting in which leadership plays out. In an extension of our discussion in chapter 3, we also will distinguish leadership amidst various demands on pastoral time and energy. We then will frame leadership specifically within the cultural dynamics of the congregation. Finally, we will relate this approach to leadership in terms of what I believe to be the pastor's ultimate goal: to help the congregation's gospel witness become and re-main dynamic.

PAUL, THE VISIONARY APOSTLE

The apostle Paul's life in ministry reveals some of leadership's basic at-tributes. For one thing, he was driven by a vision of how the gospel of Christ could make a difference in the world of his day. That vision—Paul's compelling picture of a possible future—overcame all divisions that hu-man beings could contrive.[1] It was to overcome such arguments as which church official was most important (1 Cor. 1:10–17), which form of wisdom is better (1 Cor. 1:18–25), which kind of social status is superior (1 Cor. 1:26–31), and whose Christian authority is more worthy (Gal. 1:10—2:14). More than this, however, was Paul's insistence that Jesus' witness to God created a wider meaning to the notion of "God's people." No longer was God's preference based merely on heritage, that is, of being descendants of Israel. Gentiles, who for centuries were treated by the Jews as outsiders to the promise, have equal access to God if they have faith (see Rom. 9 and 10). These convictions led Paul to stand up for and encourage Gentile converts to the way (Gal. 2:11–14; compare Acts 15).

Paul's vision of the gospel's possibilities for all groups of people led him to travel throughout the Roman world, preaching, founding, and support-ing young Gentile churches. He gave years of his life and energy to this work. Paul was a leader: He articulated and created a following for his vi-sion. The work was not easy, for the Jesus movement was young and grow-ing. There were many obstacles, even (or perhaps especially) once congregations began to form. Yet Paul was convinced that the people he could reach needed to seek to embody this vision of a new world.

THE IMPACT OF CHOICE[2]

In at least one important respect, the world in which Paul promulgated his Christian vision is similar to our modern/postmodern world. Both of these eras allowed, or even encouraged, some degree of freedom concerning re-ligious choice. The first couple of generations of the Christian movement gave prominence to features of personal choice and participation that created new structures and further encouraged others. Individuals made decisions to follow the Way; many early churches transcended racial and socioeconomic boundaries; members could gain status in the church that was not available in society; and the early church created ways of getting the Word out and constituting itself.

Centuries later, European Protestantism spawned an interest in some quarters to eliminate government's authority over the church. Wherever this movement succeeded, the volunteer church was born again—a church with which persons could choose not to be involved, that was not supported by tax money, that attended to its own matters, and thus, that created a symbol of its being free: the offering plate. This "disestablished" church opened the way for other, secular forms of free association to emerge, in spite of political and intellectual opposition to them.

This bird's-eye look at the historical development of voluntary associations helps us appreciate the meaning of leadership. In today's society, we are very aware of how many different kinds of voluntary associations exist. Each one has its particular mission and demands on those who join it. Consequently, various groups end up vying with one another for our loyalties; as James Luther Adams points out, "associations compete with each other for support."[3] Hence, when persons in our society can elect to join a group, their commitment to a "leader" is not bound by necessity; it must be earned.[4] True leaders cannot take member participation for granted; a pastor cannot rely simply on the conviction that "God called me" to head up a congregation. In order to lead, there must be followers. It takes vision for a person to propel others to lead or to follow.

EXPANDING THE MEANING OF LEADERSHIP

Indeed, leadership and vision are integrally intertwined. As Lovett Weems puts it, "Leadership exists to make possible a preferred future (vision) for the people involved. . . ."[5] In its broadest terms, this is the heart of leadership. In the context of our exploration of pastors getting along with their churches, this notion of leadership needs to be elaborated.

VISION AT THE CENTER

As we begin to frame our outlook on congregations within culture, instructive ties between culture, vision, and leadership become clearer. Let us first speak in terms from chapter 1. A vision consists of *a set of espoused values that are understood in some particular relationship with one another.* Most churches would identify certain elements of their visions as being in common, having to do with the Good News, salvation, Jesus Christ, Christian living, and so on. Yet the most useful visions also will be grounded in the context of the specific congregation—its heritage, its particular community, its way of doing theology.[6] When espoused values from all of these sources come together in a church's vision, they are configured idiosyncratically, that is, uniquely arranged for that one congregation.

Pastors become leaders when they help a congregation articulate and follow such a distinctive vision. Since vision is about something that has not completely come to be, some of the espoused values in the vision have not yet been fully tested. This means that they have not had a chance to be proven and thus transformed into some of the congregation's basic, shared assumptions. Churches who seek to integrate racially provide a vivid example of this "not yet" quality. If a congregation claims a vision to become a church for all races, one look in the sanctuary on a Sunday morning will indicate to what extent that vision is being actualized. So pastoral leadership involves attention to testing the untested values to show that they can work and thus to embed them among the congregation's deep assumptions.

A LEARNING SPIRIT

Leadership, then, also entails a relationship between the church's culture and its *ability to learn.*[7] Leadership is not simply about some strong-minded, attractive, charismatic figure who leads the charge for an inviting cause. For pastors, many of whom, over the years, move in and out of several congregations, the challenges to leadership often call for a less dramatic strategy. Especially in the rapidly changing environment of the twenty-first century, churches need to be able to respond. They need to learn how to learn, how to pay attention to what is going on around them, how to adjust their focus on the future, and how to let their shared assumptions change as a result. This set of tasks takes plenty of energy and can release lots of apprehension within the congregation, especially among the longtime members.[8] In the short run, a pastor might feel that a process like this is too risky. Yet, the risk of conflict can pay off in the long run, if the situations are handled well.[9] Pastors who are leaders understand such an opportunity and have learned the skills to work with it.

QUALITIES OF LEARNING

In other words, helping a church learn how to learn is itself an experience in enculturation.[10] Pastors who are leaders help their congregations test and prove the value that churches can keep on adapting themselves. Being able and committed to such a fundamental task calls for distinct qualities from the persons who seek to undertake it.[11] For one thing, they must possess an acumen for discerning who they are and what they bring to their dealings with their work. Pastors who have had experience outside their context of origin tend to be more aware of their assumptions. This puts them in a better position to perceive their church's circumstances more objectively.

A second quality for being an effective leader of cultural learning is willingness to figure out how to help the congregation name the truth about itself. Such willingness has to put the well-being of the congregation ahead of the pastor's personal needs and interests. Related to this quality is, third, being healthy enough to handle the consequences of putting a learning process in motion. Pastors need to be both spiritually and psychologically mature, or the pressures brought about by members' apprehensions will derail any constructive possibilities.

FOCI FOR LEARNING

These three internal qualities for the pastor as a learning leader are matched by three action qualities. One is to help the congregation develop new, shared assumptions to replace those that need to be released. Rev. Song discovered in her new appointment that one clan in the congregation held all the church positions. Other church members complained to her that they wanted to share in the authority and responsibility as well. Quietly, Rev. Song agreed. In her first year with the congregation, she politely, but clearly, stood against certain actions by the dominating clan to continue their lock on power. Subsequently, some of them resigned their positions. These developments allowed members of other church families to get involved with significant congregational duties. Rev. Song was espousing a value such as, "Church has a place for everyone to contribute in a worthwhile way to the mission." Her actions were led by this value. As other members began to get more involved in the church's work, the church was learning that this value could work; a new shared assumption was forming in their midst.

A second action quality for pastors who learn and change culture is also demonstrated in the story of Rev. Song. It is to engage church members in the process, by listening to and working with their groups and activities. A pastor is not a leader if he or she attempts to impose something on the congregation. Cultural change must occur within the congregation, not merely in the mind of the pastor. This theme of getting church members involved appears in many recent publications on church renewal.[12] Rev. Song was committed to expanding the base of member involvement, not diminishing it.

Third, the learning pastor/leader is capable of entering a new congregation and learning the culture that is there before seeking to help it change. This chapter's opening story provides a case in point. Rev. Blake recalls that she spent the first year observing the congregation, its members and activities. She sought to care for them, listening to their stories, hurts, hopes, and dreams. She was not judgmental. In this way, the Rev. Blake began to learn that tiny church's culture and how to find her way as a learning pastor.

CONTEXT AND BEING "ON THE EDGE"[13]

Defining leadership as we have done so here makes even more sense when we utilize two other culture-based concepts. One of these concepts is context, or the environment and surroundings of the congregation. Every church is located somewhere, not anywhere, and its members reside in specific places. As we saw in chapter 1, culture's complexity arises from the flowing together of many aspects of culture, as they meet in one place. A congregation's surroundings heavily influence its prospects for ministry. Thus, one key task in pastoral leadership is to pay attention to what is happening in the church's context and then consider what modifications in the church's ministry might be called for.

Sensitivity to context suggests one more quality of leadership, one that longtime pastors are especially in danger of losing. This quality is marginality. In order to give serious care to the church's context, a pastor must be able to put herself or himself, to some degree, outside of that church's culture. In other words, if the pastor is too enculturated, he or she will have lost the capacity to realize what is changing. Even more dangerous, the pastor will become incapable of recognizing that what has changed is something for the church to take into account. Marginality—being able to stand at times on the edges of the congregation's way of life—enables the pastor to keep learning.

I interviewed once for a position as associate pastor of a residential church in a large city. Once a congregation of eight hundred members, the church now had about four hundred on the rolls. Church school enrollment gradually had dwindled from four hundred to fifty. The pastor, Rev. Captain, had begun his ministry with the congregation as an assistant pastor and had served as pastor there for the last twenty years. He was devoted, hardworking, affable. Before the interview, I called someone who had served with Rev. Captain to get an idea of what he was like. When I asked the question, there was a noticeable pause before the reply. "The first thing you need to know about Rev. Captain," he said, "is that he has not had a new idea in twenty-five years." That one statement led me to approach the interview very alert to learning more—and cautious about what I would find!

LEADERSHIP CONTRASTED

This incident illustrates a crucial distinction that this chapter seeks to amplify. Pastoral leadership is not defined only by working hard, reading the Bible, praying for wisdom and guidance, winning the trust and support of the church members, preaching good sermons, and giving helpful pastoral care. I hope that a pastor who leads does all of these things! Yet, a pastor can "do all the right things" and still not be leading the congregation. As Lovett Weems points out, "doing the right things" is the focus of management, while "doing things right" is the focus of administration. Administration deals with what needs to be taken care of on a day-to-day basis. Management looks to mid-range matters such as planning. Leadership will encompass both administration and management, but it is more. In Weems' words, "Leadership is the development and articulation of a shared vision, motivation . . . and . . . cooperation. . . ." [14]

Pastors become leaders when they attend to operational matters (administration) and oversight issues (management) with their eyes constantly fixed on a vision for their congregations. The sad truth is that pastors who never have new ideas never will become leaders. This will be the case as well with any other office or position in the church that someone fills, whether it be as elder, deacon, Christian education director, minister of music, or anything else. Leadership keeps the big picture in focus and acts upon it.

LEADERSHIP AS CULTURAL CHANGE

Let us now be explicit about one claim that emerges from this approach to defining leadership. Inevitably, a pastor who leads will trigger change in a congregation's culture. This phenomenon of change in culture is so important to understand because so much is at stake. Remember that culture is not bad in itself; in fact, culture exists in part because human communities require a certain amount of stability in order to survive and thrive. Leadership is necessary especially when the community's context begins to alter. This is the case because the shared assumptions undergirding the culture, which proved reliable at an earlier time, could become less useful as the context changes. A pastoral leader recognizes that all three layers of the congregation's culture will be involved in change—the artifacts, the espoused values, and the shared, basic assumptions.

LEVELS OF INTERACTION

Let us see how the three levels interact when change comes into play. Remember first that the church's artifacts are easy to notice, but difficult to understand. Say, for instance, that an Episcopalian attends worship on a Sunday morning and then accompanies a friend for the first time to a Pentecostal prayer meeting on Sunday night. The Episcopalian will observe that many objects, spaces, rituals, and so on in the Pentecostal church bear some resemblance to her home-church experience. People assemble in a room with religious symbols (though there perhaps will be fewer of them in the Pentecostal church); there is music with instruments and songbooks; a few selected persons "up front" lead parts of the service; passages of scripture are read; prayers are offered; and so on.

However, it more likely will be what appears different to the Episcopalian guest that will make the deeper impression on her. What is familiar is mingled with what is new: different music and songs, more expressive and higher-volume behavior; speaking in tongues; an altar call; and other things. If the Episcopalian were using the language of the three layers of culture, she would reflect on the prayer service something like this: "I saw a number of artifacts that I recognized and some that were familiar but also different. It got me to thinking that there must be some distinctions in the espoused values and shared assumptions between our two congregations. My church's worship style tends to value order and serenity; his seems to value spontaneity and action. I need to ask questions, and observe more of its activity, in order to understand better the deeper levels of this religious culture."

LEVELS AND CHANGE

An experience like this one would point out that new pastors (or new staff or church members, for that matter) cannot presume to know the meaning that an unfamiliar church gives to its own artifacts. Similarly, it reminds us that, because artifacts are intricately tied in with the congregation's values and assumptions, creating change in the church involves all three levels of culture. Pastors who are leaders need to take seriously the idea that simply talking about something new (espoused value) does not make it happen. Ironically, though, doing something new (artifact) will not necessarily guarantee a positive change in the church, either.

In leading a congregation, pastors account for the three levels of culture. Yet, the way in which the three levels interact in any congregation does not remain static. Newer, younger churches deal with different cultural issues than well-established or weakening churches. It is incumbent on the pastor to understand these differences, but it is even more important to know what pastoral leadership's ultimate goal for the congregation looks like. Let us conclude this chapter on leadership with a concise presentation of an organizational model that helps pastors know where to head their churches.

LEADING FOR A DYNAMIC, VITAL CHURCH

Pastors play a key role in helping congregation either to attain, sustain, or regain vitality. If we acknowledge that congregations go through various phases throughout their existence, the distinctions in leadership strategy called for from pastors make a lot of sense.[15] Younger congregations are still in flux and depend on their pastor to help them attain the dynamic features that make ministry most effective. Established churches, ones that feel settled in and confident about their place in the world, need their pastors to help them maintain their vision—to keep it fresh—so that the tail does not wag the dog. Weakening congregations, by contrast, need a pastor who can tap into forgotten energy and regain their vitality in ministry.

There is a fairly simple, yet very useful, way to analyze your church's place along its life cycle. This four-function model builds here on its introduction in chapter 3. As a practical tool, this model gives you as pastor a basic road map for moving your church forward. This model will serve you well, whether your congregation needs to attain, sustain, or regain the vitality that makes its ministry most potent. Let us elaborate on each of the four functions, discuss their interplay, and see how pastoral leadership can help a congregation stay dynamic.

THE FOUR FUNCTIONS[16]

Every organization—every business, government agency, professional association, church, or other organization—is pivotally influenced by four factors. These are not optional; by the very nature of being organized, all organizations in our era must account for the what, the who, the how, and the why of their existence. What makes organizational life interesting is that the four functions do not necessarily get along with one another! Each one demands something different, thus creating an inherent tug-of-war within the church. The tug-of-war itself is normal; how it is handled makes all the difference in whether the church achieves that important dynamic stage.

Perform. The *what* function refers to all the activities and programs of the congregation. Churches do things. They gather regularly to sing, pray, and worship and to share fellowship with each other, to study and learn, to assist those in need, and to help their communities become healthy places for everyone. It takes time and energy for a church to do things. This function demands much attention.

Relate. Doing things means involving people, which leads to the *who* function. Yet "who" is more subtle than simply accounting for the congregation's members, staff, and those who might become members. It is even more nuanced than acknowledging the residents and property owners around your church's facility or the municipal agencies that have some say in what you do—or any other potential or actual constituency of your congregation. "Who" encompasses all of these categories, but it also has to do with the sense of belonging that characterizes your church. Deep in its bones, whom does the congregation actually treat as "one of us"? People who look like you, dress and talk like you, live near you, and like you? People who have been members of the church the longest? "Who" acts as the church's "glue": It reveals who and how the church sticks together.[17]

Execute. Churches, then, do things with people. They also do things certain ways. This third function, *how*, takes in the processes and structures (both formal and informal ones) that a church develops in order to put resources to work for its "what" and "who" functions. Some church traditions impose a certain structure of boards and offices for each one of their parishes, such as a Session or Council, elders, deacons, trustee boards, and so on.

Ideally, these structures function as they are intended. However, within (and sometimes in spite of!) these formal arrangements can develop informal, idiosyncratic ways of getting things done. These kinds of unofficial "how" processes often dominate in small and rural congregations and become lodged with long-standing members. Even if such members do not hold important offices for years, their influence on the church can over-shadow the authority vested in the offices themselves. The board of trust-ees never crosses Aunt Minnie, who looks after the kitchen with great care. Mr. Bolden is retired and has done repairs on the building for years, with-out anyone asking. Regardless of what combination of formal and infor-mal processes actually work in your church, the fact remains that this function of "how" is necessary.

Envision. Experienced pastors know that these first three functions (what, who, and how) can clash with each other. Church members who are con-cerned about propriety ("how") might become impatient with a pastor who is more concerned about making things happen ("what"). A new pas-tor who is attracting new members could discover that it is not easy to help these new members assimilate into the current membership ("who"). Per-haps the most strenuous clashes, however, can occur between any one of these three functions and the fourth one.

This fourth function is called *why*, because it has to do with the church's purpose or vision.[18] Every church has to have a reason to exist, and one of the most serious situations into which churches put themselves is in allow-ing their vision to become weak. Often this occurs once a church has passed its glory days and is coasting on its laurels. Vision is so crucial to a congre-gation—and thus to pastoral leadership—because it provides the energy to drive the other three functions. When a church has identified a clear and compelling vision for itself, decisions about the other functions begin to fall into place. "What do we do as a church?" Look at your vision for guid-ance. "Who should be involved?" What is your vision seeking to accom-plish with people? "How should we go about our business?" Let the decisions about structures and processes be shaped by your what and who, not the other way around. And let all decisions begin with the vision.

LEADING TOWARD VITALITY

This four-part model of a congregation helps us see what pastors need to do in order to be leaders. The strongest culture that your church can achieve is the one in which its vision provides authentic impetus for everything the church does. This is what I mean by a "vital, dynamic" congregation. You want your church to learn how to reach this point and keep itself there. In order to do so, the congregation has to learn how to learn. That is possible only if you, their pastor, teach them how. A church with a learning culture is able to be proactive when it sees changes around itself.[19] Otherwise, it will lose its cutting edge, its strong vision, and gradually end up with a weak culture. Weak cultures require skilled energy to lead, because the pastor cannot (as we saw, for instance, in chapter 2) force it to change.

Pastors who are leaders put their energy into helping their congregations keep why, what, who, and how in a creative relationship. This is another way to describe the dynamic, vital stage that will best serve the church. Getting to that stage, however, is a process all its own. Many churches first will need to *get* there, or get *back* there, before they can learn how to *stay* there. Actually, staying in a dynamic stage is a process in itself, which means that learning continues.

Pastor Blake, from our opening story, led her assigned congregation from weakness to vital, dynamic strength. In those years with that church, she acted as a leader, whether she realized it or not. For that, we can give thanks to God! If we visited that church five years later, what would we observe? If Rev. Blake was still pastor there, what might she be doing? Would she still be a learning pastor? Would the congregation be learning how to learn? What would they have noticed in their community? What changes might they have made because of their learning? How might their culture be different as a result?

We would hope that Pastor Blake would have kept on learning herself and taught the church how to learn. One of the greatest marks of pastoral leadership is to leave a church that is healthy and dynamic and knows how to keep itself fresh in Christian witness. In previous chapters, we have explored what it takes to develop the cultural capital to be in a position for the pastoral leadership that we have outlined here. In the following chapter, we will explore the intricacies of threats to that cultural capital. Pastor-church disagreements can be handled to the good of the church's witness, if you understand the nature of the cultural beast.

Handling Conflict

What If Things Go Sour?

AVOIDING A SHOWDOWN

PASTOR TENNYSON HAD COME to the conclusion, very reluctantly, that it was time for him to go. Having pastored St. Matthew Church for fourteen years, the conscientious Rev. Tennyson had served through three presidential elections and a war that was followed by unparalleled economic prosperity. The membership of the parish had nearly doubled during his tenure, while its reputation (based on its having been the first parish in town) remained strong. New residents sought out St. Matthew's because of its activities, programs, and civic involvement. For the most part, Pastor Tennyson had felt good about this congregation.

Yet trouble was brewing. The church was running out of room. Their facility was only twenty years old, but classrooms and fellowship events of late always were crowded. The trustees of St. Matthew's had proposed construction of a new sanctuary and conversion of the present building to expanded program space (for instance, the Boy Scouts needed more room for their supplies). The trustees' plan was shared at a meeting of the parish, but it was not until the next church council meeting that signs of dissent surfaced. These were aimed at the good pastor. Certain council members reported, from certain church members, misgivings over whether Rev. Tennyson had the capacity for overseeing a major building campaign successfully. In spite of these voiced concerns, that night the council unanimously passed a resolution in support of their pastor.

Just a week later, a meeting of the entire congregation was held. It had to be specially called because a few days earlier Pastor Tennyson had submitted a letter of resignation. He was distressed by the show of discontent concerning his pastoral leadership. He might have been wondering if his decision six years ago to stay with St. Matthew's had been a wise one. At that time, another church in a distant city had asked him to be a candidate for their head of staff position. Rev. Tennyson had traveled to that city, interviewed with the other church, and was offered the job, which came with a hefty increase in compensation package. He hardly had returned home before news of his impending departure had leaked out to the congregation. Quickly, the church council assembled and agreed to meet the other church's package. Rev. Tennyson took that action as a sign that he should stay with St. Matthew's.

Now it was too late for him to second-guess that choice. The parish membership was convening to act on his letter of resignation. Telephone conversations between St. Matthew's members had been thick and furious over the last several days. What had they discussed about Rev. Tennyson's actions and style as a pastor? What was the tone of their exchanges? What would they decide to do? Did Pastor Tennyson need to go?

THE NASTY "C" WORD

Does this story sound familiar? Have you, or a pastor whom you know, ever endured circumstances in your church like this one? Have you ever left a called or appointed position under a cloud? How did that experience leave you feeling, about yourself, about the church in question, about your denomination's role—about pastoral ministry itself?

Publicly, pastors and churches tend not to want to talk about their experiences with conflict. They want others to see them as successful, capable, and pleasant to work with. Pastors and churches prefer to keep any such painful events in the closet, hidden from view. They would rather put their best foot forward, put on their best face, and put the past behind them.

It is never that easy. Relationships between pastors and congregations can go sour, and they sometimes do. In fact, judging by the stories that I have heard over the past twenty-five years, pastor-church conflict seems to be on a dramatic rise. So it might surprise you to know that the story of Pastor Tennyson and St. Matthew's Church, which is true, took place many decades ago, in the 1920s! That experience those many years ago should reassure those of us who carry the banner of Christian faith into the twenty-first century. As painful as they might be, our pastoral experiences with church conflict are not anything new.

NEW TESTAMENT SNAPSHOT

As we might expect, the theme of pastors struggling with their congregations has its parallels in the Scriptures. Neither is it surprising that some of the most revealing sources are from the letters of the apostle Paul. A small section, two verses long, at the beginning of 1 Corinthians seems to capture the essence of the challenge of conflict that churches face. Verse 10 reads: "Now I appeal to you, brothers and sisters, by the name of our Lord Jesus Christ, that all of you be in agreement and that there be no divisions among you, but that you be united in the same mind and the same purpose."

Sounds wonderful, doesn't it? A church with unity of thought and purpose, where members do not split into factions! We know that this is an ideal that many congregations find very difficult to approach. Paul saw it coming in his day; verse 11 reads: "For it has been reported to me by Chloe's people that there are quarrels among you, my brothers and sisters." Perish the thought! Quarrels? It can't be! Not in those pristine, ideal first years of the Jesus movement! Christians not getting along—in church? Christians are not supposed to fight!

Well, those of us with a few years of pastoral experience under our belts know that Christians do not always get along. We also know that pastors not infrequently end up in the middle of such contests. New Testament witnesses to conflict reveal a variety of circumstances that create conflict. Not all of them put religious leaders at the front of the lines, but it is difficult for pastors, other ministers, Christian education directors, and others to avoid getting pulled into the fray.

IN THIS CHAPTER

In a moment, we will look a little closer at themes of conflict in the New Testament and contemporary attempts to deal with church conflict. Because of the scope of both subjects, our purpose here is not to cover all those topics and models of strategy. Having some orientation to them, however, will help us more clearly locate the particular approach of this chapter. We will seek to gain fresh insight into episodes of church tension in which the pastor is identified as a central player. This topic distinguishes the present chapter from chapter four, when we discussed the role of the pastor in helping the congregation face difficult circumstances that tend to force their way. Surely the two topics overlap, yet they are not always the same.

In this chapter, therefore, we will be framing the matter of struggles between pastor and church in terms of culture and cultural capital. Our goal first will be to see this tense yet common phenomenon through the cultural perspective being utilized in this book. A new viewpoint makes it possible to create new, constructive ways to respond. For one thing, this chapter opens up a way to avoid, in many situations, having to assign blame. Turning pastor-church conflict away from "witch-hunting" provides more useful options for resolving the predicament. We will discover and outline some strategies that cultural-capital analysis suggests. The pastor's own assessment of cultural capital within the congregation becomes a key factor to a healthy response and subsequently a productive outcome.

BRIMMING WITH CONFLICT POTENTIAL

Pastors know too well that they easily can be swept into the center of the parish's frictions and antagonisms. She or he might not have "started" them, but all it takes for the pastor to enter the ring is a member's perception of the pastor contributing to the escalation. As suggested above, the New Testament literature points to a number of kinds of conflict that can affect a congregation. Being aware of what some of these conflicts look like offers some level of "fair warning" to astute pastors.

Carl Dudley and Earle Hilgert, in their illuminating study of "tensions" in the New Testament, organize their evidence around a few key categories.[1] The earliest Christian congregations faced challenges first as they created community.[2] They had to agree on terminology and symbols that would express their image of the Christian calling. On the one hand, they grappled over their delicate but intense experience of fellowship while, on the other hand, seeking to develop stability over the long haul. Early Christians also discovered that it was not easy to find a satisfactory way to live in the wider society. They became countercultural, wrestling in different locations and generations to establish an appropriate relationship with the massive, ancient population of peasantry, sometimes empowering it, other times limiting it.[3]

We also see through Dudley and Hilgert's research contests emerging in New Testament churches over the nature of the faith itself.[4] What evangelistic appeal could be used with unbelievers? How was the death of Jesus to be understood in the purposes of God? How were Christians to understand and deal with the anticipated "last things," when they did not occur as first expected? In the New Testament, there are no single answers to these and similar questions.

This overview helps us appreciate the complexity of life that emerges within today's parishes; it also underscores the idea that tension and disagreement are practically inherent. Dudley and Hilgert argue that tensions like these force a congregation into "recognizing its humanity."[5] They also propose that evidence from New Testament churches alludes to certain features that were used constructively: showing regard for persons, talking through the problems, relating the need for resolution to the call for wider Christian witness, and so on.[6]

It would be hard to find fault with such positive features as these! So let us see how we can put ourselves into a better position to apply such features by understanding our church's cultural capital. A review of some of the previous material will help us discover avenues of resolution.

THE CONGREGATION AS CULTURE

Earlier in this book, we discussed a number of concepts that paint a landscape of culture for the stage of our congregational drama. These concepts were grouped in categories such as levels, layers, dimensions, and phases. Taken together, these concepts give us practical tools for analyzing and interpreting the behavior of our congregations in a way that reveals their amazing richness and depth. As pastors, we might not always like what we discover. Yet the alternative—trying to function in a congregation without adequate knowledge or insight—courts disaster.

A parish's richness and depth begin with its three levels of culture: the artifacts; the espoused values; and the shared, basic assumptions. We have already applied these three concepts to the task of the pastor entering a congregation's life for the first time. There is no way that a pastor can know the parish's assumptions, and know which ones relate directly with its espoused values, without immersing himself or herself into that parish's activities and people. These assumptions, which drive the congregation in an almost unconscious way, originate from an almost dizzying host of sources.

Culture is even more subtle than this. We also were introduced to several layers by which culture forms: macro-, meso- (several kinds), micro-, sub-, and organizational. We also looked briefly at the ways in which a congregation's culture changes throughout its life cycle. As these various concepts described a multitude of aspects of culture, we began to appreciate the kaleidoscopic way in which culture impinges its attributes upon us. Indeed, we spoke of the local church in terms of a "confluence of culture," where so many streams of culture flow together in one place. Perhaps more than any other kind of organization, today's voluntary congregations comprise cultural confluence in its most idiosyncratic forms. It is hard to imagine any other place where so much looks familiar yet so much can be unexpectedly different.

Hence, in this book, it is through such an intricate, kaleidoscopic lens that we view our churches. Our approach to understanding church-pastor conflict here will be distinct from other, previous interpretations, in which culture was less of an explicit tool.[7] One main advantage that cultural interpretation provides is a bigger picture, a way to see more of the stage on which the drama of conflict gets played out. This advantage should not be underestimated, for the better you know what is going on, the more fittingly your strategy can be shaped.

CREATING CONFLICT IN ONE EASY STEP

Unfortunately, it often is easier for a new pastor to create conflict than to avoid it. One young Methodist pastor found out this truism rather quickly. He had just graduated from seminary and was appointed to a very small parish in a rural community in Georgia. Arriving there a few days before his first worship service, the eager graduate drove by the church building. It was very old, somewhat decrepit and, to the parish's new pastor, in violation of fire codes. An old gnarly tree off to the side of the structure virtually prevented use of the only side door. Clearly, here was a moment to prove himself, the pastor thought.

Driving to the church parsonage, he unpacked some things until he found his chain saw. He returned to the church building and immediately cut down the tree, cleaned up the limbs and twigs, and painted the door. In less than a week, this brand new pastor was heading off to a different appointment. Why? Because of that tree. It was an old tree, all right, almost two hundred years of age. Seems that a special foreign visitor had planted it when Georgia was quite young. The visitor's name? None other than England's John Wesley, founder of the Methodist movement![8]

If ever there was a story that illustrated so many elements of the importance of congregational culture, this one does so. If ever a pastor moved so quickly to create conflict in the congregation, this pastor would win the booby prize! He caused a furor before he even met any of the church members. Without any knowledge of their history, their artifacts, or espoused values (to say nothing of their deep, shared assumptions), this new pastor violated the parish's culture. Having been raised in the American macroculture that values efficiency and a "take-charge" style, the pastor quickly came to the wrong conclusions. It never occurred to him that there was a special, local reason for the tree's long presence, in spite of its appearance and menacing location. Since he consulted with no one, he allowed no opportunity for himself to learn.

ZERO BALANCE IN THE CULTURE BANK

The pastor who cut down the Wesley tree created a conflict so quickly in his brand-new parish because he had not developed any cultural capital in it. Virtually the only things that he knew about it were its location and the condition of its modest facilities. The only knowledge that the parish had about him was whatever the district superintendent passed on. Being rural, small, and isolated, the parish probably had given up long ago having high hopes about any of its new pastors. As a heavily oral culture, the parish would have been ready to extend him their brand of hospitality.[9] Yet, as is often the case, the new pastor perceived the situation in terms of the literate, professional culture that college and seminary studies emphasized.[10] He did not give them a chance to know him and, thus, learn to trust him. He had invested little in that parish which, in this case, was the wrong kind of action to invest.

Because of this, the pastor had nothing on which to draw when the parish realized what he had done. The metaphor of capital helps us see the problem. When he arrived in town, the pastor's cultural capital with the new parish was almost zero. This is completely understandable, since they had had no association yet. When the parish members found out what their new pastor had done, his cultural capital with them immediately shot into the red deficit column. Why? Because his action destroyed a proud, albeit awkward, symbol of their culture—the Wesley tree. The parish had so much of their cultural identity invested in that tree that it would have taken a tremendous amount of cultural capital on the pastor's part to overcome the offense. Yet, since he had just arrived, the pastor had none of the cultural capital he needed. The conflict was resolved probably the best way that it could have been, for the long run.

Some of my seminary students, on hearing this story, have argued that the parish had a responsibility to mark the Wesley tree in a way that would ensure that newcomers would respect its heritage. To a formally educated, literate thinker, this solution seems reasonable. Within the life of that rural community's oral culture, however, such a proposal would not occur to them. Within their life together, history and meaning are passed on by word of mouth. As they assume it, everyone in town already knows! Outsiders are infrequent and temporary, and their idiosyncrasies can be tolerated for a time. It never occurred to anyone that a new pastor would arrive and remove one of their church's most precious artifacts.

CHURCH CONFLICT: CULTURAL INTERPRETATIONS

The story of the Wesley tree places in dramatic relief the way in which cultural interpretation of a congregation can be used to understand conflict. For one thing, conflict can occur if the pastor steps on one of the church's cultural land mines (i.e., their shared assumptions). Perhaps you have heard other pastors say, as I have, "I never saw that one coming, but now I wish that I had." Remember the young pastor who suggested not replacing the American flag in the sanctuary? Even though he had been the church's pastor for five years, he misinterpreted the value of that symbol to the dominant subculture of the congregation. When he spoke with me about the incident a week later, he was still shell-shocked from having stepped on that land mine!

"Not seeing it coming" is probably the most common way that conflict around pastors emerges. As such, it catches everyone by surprise, generating a level of distress that would bring pause to an outsider. Yet, conflict around pastors also can emerge when the pastor takes a calculated risk. There might be a project in which the pastor is personally committed but for which the congregation might not share interest. A pastor who is aware of this difference of interest might go ahead and take action, hoping that the church will come around.

An urban pastor once was living in a small parsonage, waiting for the parish to complete a larger house for his occupancy. Just about the time that he could begin moving, the pastor became aware of an immigrant family from Southeast Asia who had nowhere to live. Without consulting anyone in the parish or parish board, this pastor invited the family to live in the older, smaller parsonage that he was vacating. Within the week, parishioners discovered the situation, and many of them were upset. Their neighborhood recently had undergone a significant racial change, and the parish was not growing. Many of the upset members had helped charter the parish and were afraid that introducing one more racial dynamic to their situation would spell the end of their church as they knew it. The pastor tried to use the opportunity to argue for the Christian faith's call to do justice and love kindness. His appeal fell on deaf ears.

Regardless of our empathy for this pastor's Christian motivation, we can see that his judgment in proceeding as he did heightened the potential for conflict. He probably felt the need to move quickly, but he could have sought support for the idea from an influential church member who trusted him. With an advocate from within the congregation's culture, the refugee housing idea would have stood a stronger chance of being accepted. Barring such approval, however, the pastor still might have been able, in a respectful way, to stimulate a conversation in practical theology among the parish. Temporary housing could have been arranged long enough for the parish to decide how it wanted to respond to the need. The pastor's role in this kind of scenario thus would be to foster the discussion, the theological reflection, and hence to "midwife" the parish's own decision.

CHURCH CONFLICT: CULTURAL SYMBOLISM

Whether a pastor creates conflict "on purpose" or not, the reality remains one of culture put to the test. As such, every potential conflict becomes a symbol within that congregation's life. Therefore, when the pastor first becomes aware of a whiff of conflict, the first thought in her or his mind should not be something like "What is their problem?" or "They must not be true believers." The former statement tends to frame the situation in psychological terms, which defines behavior along the lines of sanity or mental health. The latter statement tends to frame the situation in potentially negative theological or spiritual language: The other person is portrayed as a questionable Christian, since they disagree with you, their pastor.

Both psychological and theological or spiritual framing are easy ways for pastors to frame disagreements they have with their churches. Neither of these frames, however, will help pastors tap into the deeper, cultural energy that is at work in the church, for theology is always clothed in culture. A more insightful question to ask at the onset of a potential crisis is, "What does this say about our church right now?" This question affords the pastor a chance to back up, to begin looking beyond the details to the larger picture. In some of the language of this book, the pastor can begin to see the circumstances as artifacts, certain parts of the discourse as espoused values, and opposition or uncertainty as obtuse symbols of some of the church's shared assumptions.

Often potential conflict in a church triggers thinking and conversation that, at least, begins to partly reveal some of the congregation's deeply held, mostly unconscious views about things. Since by their nature these assumptions develop out of the church's experience and are not subject to the rationality of a voting process, it often takes a threatening action to help members articulate them. These assumptions then are expressed in negative terms as a way to oppose the threat. An astute observer would be able to restate these negative-sounding assumptions in positive, more palatable and constructive, language.

One main reason that church conflict gets confusing is because assumptions are at stake and their power is symbolic. Newer members in the congregation might not be able to figure out "what all the fuss is about" until they have heard some of the older stories called on to explain why this or that should or should not be done. Church disagreement surely is symbolic and at its root is the matter of vision. When conflict erupts, regardless of what point along its life cycle a church currently exists, vision stands ultimately to be defended, amended, or upended. At its heart, then, church conflict becomes, often unknowingly, a contest between visions, the preferred one versus a(n implicitly) proposed one.

SYMBOLISM AND UNEARTHING SHARED ASSUMPTIONS

We have argued that the three levels of culture help us appreciate the complexity that emerges within pastor-church disagreements. Being able to unearth the shared assumptions that are being triggered by the disagreement opens the way for a thoughtful and more spiritual tone for resolving things. Below, we will look at some statements expressing assumptions that appear, from my observations, to be fairly common among congregations. These statements should help you get a better idea of what you as a pastor are looking for when storm clouds begin to appear on the horizon of your church.

Before considering these statements, though, it will be useful also to remind ourselves about how perplexing it can be to determine the sources of shared assumptions. Since we are discussing churches, we might presume that their assumptions are all religious and doctrinal in nature. This is not the case. Congregations arise out of particular contexts and continue to be affected by many elements of those contexts. Even though the presence of these elements is often not acknowledged in congregational discourse, they nonetheless are very instrumental.

CORPORATE AMERICA

One common source of assumptions in our American macroculture is the hierarchical, bureaucratic model of organizations.[11] Position descriptions, chain of command, complex accounting systems, competition for market share, annual reviews, and the like all have become familiar features of the operation of many congregations. They have been borrowed from the corporate world of the twentieth century, which gave rise to the most complex organizations the world has ever seen. Because this kind of structure—and the cultural values it generates—is so pervasive still today, our churches are affected by it. Pastors often try to get into the largest church they can and "work their way up" during their careers. Churches sometimes treat staff, including pastors, as easily replaceable parts, to be discarded if they "don't work out right." Values and practices from corporate America have been imbedded in many of our congregations and denominational structures.

LEGAL WRANGLING

So also is the case for the litigious nature of the United States. Americans seem to sue one another at the drop of a hat. Whenever a disagreement occurs, or something goes wrong, lawsuits and legal maneuverings become the order of the day. A congregation dominated by professionals in its membership can expect to resort to legal-type practices. Sometimes these practices help, other times they harm the congregation.

SPORTS AND ENTERTAINMENT

In the latter third of the twentieth century, we saw a tremendous rise in forms of audience-oriented recreation. Not only have professional sports leagues multiplied, but also have the ways in which people can merely sit and watch something. Electronic technologies continue to develop increasingly sophisticated systems for watching videos, chatting with persons online across the globe, listening to music, and playing simulation games. A generation and more of American adults has no knowledge of living without television and programs like *Sesame Street*. These forms of entertainment often compete with local churches for people's commitments and interests. They also affect what people expect a church to "do for them," in "meeting my needs."

INDIVIDUALISM

Recently, I asked two African students in one of my classes to share with the other students insights from their vantage point about being effective as a pastor. Both of them spoke about the importance of understanding the culture that the pastor enters. One of them, for instance, spoke of how, as a young pastor, he visited an older woman in the parish and declined her offer of tea when he arrived. When she replied, "Then we will have none of your prayers," the African pastor relented, drank some tea, and then was able to continue with his pastoral visit. He concluded by exhorting his classmates to be sensitive to cultural practices within the parish.

A younger student in the class was not pleased to hear such talk. He argued against the point, citing experiences of his own in which he felt put upon by the expectations of a group. Other students tried to help the younger student see what his African colleagues meant, but he was not persuaded. Finally, as though exasperated by the entire dialogue, he asked, "But what about my rights as an individual?"

This young student minister articulated one of the most taken-for-granted assumptions of American society. It is that each one of us is inherently entitled to live as we wish, to choose without imposition from the group. This assertion of individualism is strong in our country, perhaps stronger than anywhere and at any time in history. Primary interest in oneself and one's wishes and wants fuels our capitalistic economy. It should surprise none of us, then, that individualism runs deep within our congregations. The "needs" of particular persons at times in a parish can come to odds with the rhythm and life of that parish. These situations will be sources of conflict.

Business, law, entertainment, and individualism all play powerful roles in American macroculture. They are among a number of sources that help shape the assumptions undergirding the cultures of our churches. Sound complicated? It certainly can be, especially if we neglect giving culture its due.

Let us now consider several assumptions that could be embedded in your church's culture. These are assumptions that might be triggered by a disagreement between pastors and their churches.

TRIGGERED ASSUMPTIONS IN CONFLICT

Christians don't fight. For many church members, the thought of their colleagues carrying on as though a war must be won appears distasteful at best. They look at espoused values from the Scriptures, such as "Love your neighbor as yourself," and try to take them seriously. They cannot imagine that people who are members of the same parish deliberately would stir up antagonism toward each other. Yet, when pastors and churches disagree, it is not easy for "Love one another" to overcome the tendency of our macroculture to compete and win.

One significant variation of this assumption is, "Pastors don't fight." A burden and responsibility that pastors carry is the expectation that their behavior should be aboveboard. Church members might lose their cool and do something hurtful; staff members might act out of a desire to protect themselves and further their careers. As much as we would hope that such behavior would not occur, we hope even more that it does not happen with pastors. Church people, and even society at large, expect from pastors a higher degree of integrity.[12] So when a pastor conducts himself or herself in a way that the congregation questions, conflict could be just around the corner. Furthermore, if a pastor appears angry or devious, this assumption, "Pastors don't fight," could be seriously violated.

We decide how much power the pastor has. In Methodist traditions, pastors itinerate—they move at the behest of their bishop, based on the needs of all the congregations in the district or conference. As I suggested in chapter 2, when pastors move frequently, it is more difficult for them to develop the cultural capital to promote significant new things. It is my contention that many parishes in appointment traditions (Episcopal included) develop shared assumptions limiting the authority and power of their pastors. These shared assumptions grow out of the congregation's experience of having to develop means of constructive continuity amidst the rhythm of changing pastoral appointments.

Recognizing this "built-in" limitation of pastors in some churches should not, however, be interpreted strictly in negative terms. It is indeed realistic for churches whose pastors come and go to learn to trust themselves first. What creates potential conflict, then, arises from pastoral behavior that the church views as an overstepping of boundaries. When a church begins to feel threatened, it very likely might express its assumptions in contentious ways.

Pastors in call traditions are not immune from stepping on this land mine, either. As I pointed out in chapter 2, a congregation's shared assumptions are not on its radar most of the time. They exist more like the deepest, widest part of an iceberg, the part that is least susceptible to breaking under contact or pressure. New pastors hardly can be expected to know these assumptions. Yet if they do something that the church's culture reserves for some other player, it does not matter whether the church is Methodist or Baptist. Conflict could quickly brew!

Our secrets should stay that way. As recounted in chapter 4, Rev. Jones blew the whistle on the trusted church treasurer who had embezzled a very large sum of money from the church's accounts. At the time, this hardworking pastor did not realize that the clannish network of multigenerational members who controlled the congregation's dominant subculture valued saving face over public exposure. Rev. Jones's initiative to handle the crisis was perceived by that network of members as exposing an embarrassing secret. Instead of running the process himself, Rev. Jones could have figured out a way to let key culture-bearers of the power network decide what to do. They could have developed their own strategy for eliciting a confession, mapping out a restitution plan, and involving civic authorities. This way, the dominant subculture's concern for secrecy, protecting members of the old guard, and maintaining a positive community image could have been balanced with other needs. This shared assumption thus would not have been violated. Involving key members would help create conditions in which they would be more likely to name their own truth, warts and all. Then the pastor can stay out of the line of fire.

We have nowhere else in life for things to go our way. Many churches grow up learning that they exist outside circles of status and influence. There are macrocultural and mesocultural factors that affect this kind of marginality. For African Americans, for instance, the legacy of slavery and oppression still looms. Historically, their congregations and denominations have been the only available haven from white-controlled structures of all kinds.[13] Similar experiences also shape other racial/ethnic groups in America, as well as working-class communities in urban areas and economically marginal rural communities.

Historical and social factors such as race, class, and location provide some of the streams from which any particular congregation creates its life. Being contextual, these factors tend to create a landscape of parameters for the churches that appear in their midst. In this case, a landscape of marginality offers fewer opportunities available to those in its shadow. It is no wonder, then, that the churches in such settings will tend to develop shared assumptions that reflect such (sometimes harsh) confines.

Pastors of churches that are oppressed or limited in stark ways need to be alert to how these limits could trigger conflict. Part of the gospel message promises hope, opportunity, and participation to peoples of low worldly regard (see, for instance, Luke 1:46–55; 1 Cor. 1:26–30). For small churches, poor churches, ethnic churches, gay churches, and others, having a place for persons to "be somebody" is paramount. If the pastor behaves in a way that appears to be undermining the membership's chance to participate, she or he could be about to step on a cultural land mine.

Similarly, a pastor in such churches is in particular danger of being pulled into "turf wars" between members. What at first might appear to be a petty spat between two people who want something their way could turn out to be a symbol of integrity. Again, when daily life offers little but shame, the church becomes the arena where disenfranchised people can accomplish something.

Might makes right. Our competitive macroculture fuels the idea that whoever has the power gets to make the rules. Some congregations, especially those not dominated by a clan, have learned from their experience that conflict gets resolved by whoever can flex the most muscle. As with other possible shared assumptions, it could be easily argued that this one has nothing to do with the gospel. It promotes instead the kind of power that the cross was intended to overcome. Be that as it may, our congregations are no less susceptible to having learned such an assumption. Pastors in these churches might be horrified to watch power plays unfold, especially when the pastor seeks to "be decent" about whatever is being contested.

Like a machine, we replace defective parts. Churches that exist in a context heavily influenced by conventional corporate practices often have high-powered practices of their own. Unlike oral cultures, these corporate-model churches value efficiency more than long-term relationships. The congregation is almost viewed like a machine, where each part has its preassigned duty. If a staff person does not perform according to plan, he or she is like a defective part that must be replaced. Assistant or associate pastors are especially prone to be treated this way in corporate-model congregations. We could protest all we want about its insensitivity, but that objection would not replace this shared assumption with a more humane and Christian one overnight.

This look at versions of some church shared assumptions should help you begin to see several ways in which pastors can get tangled in church conflict. Make no mistake: A pastor has to contend with shared assumptions all the time. As we have seen in earlier chapters, learning to decipher and work with assumptions is one of a pastor's key tasks. This chapter suggests how a failure to do so can create problems, for the pastor and the congregation.

REFRAME, NOT BLAME

Cultural interpretation thus provides a way to reduce the tension in church conflict. If attention is given to understanding the deeper issues at stake, concern for who is "right" and "wrong" takes a back seat to the more important matter of what the church stands to lose or gain. Would it not be a breath of grace to be able to sit together—pastor, staff, church officials, members—and seek understanding free of the onus of culpability? How much better could each person participate, learn, appreciate others, and help solve the common needs.

This cultural approach does not at all eliminate the part that individual responsibility and accountability plays in working through disagreement. Rather, it locates these factors within the larger arena of the congregation's life and cultural dynamics. Too many churches have long histories of running out pastors or uncooperative church members because it was easier to blame one person than to see what was happening within the church.

Admittedly, teaching a church to approach its disagreements in such a manner will take time and energy. Training when the church is not under tension will help parish officials be ready to lead the dynamics more fruitfully. If some pastors and church members think that it is too difficult to learn to "fight" differently, I would ask them only to remember other church conflicts about which they know. In the long run, when the church looks to scapegoat its problems, no one wins. Pastors, church officials, church members, and the parish itself all suffer deeply. The vitality of the Christian witness is too much to gamble on poor response to disagreement.

CULTURAL STRATEGIES FOR CONFLICT

Now that we have tasted some ways in which pastor-church conflict can arise, let us turn to the practical matter of pastoral strategy. A cultural-capital model helps us understand in any given conflict situation what our options are. We first will look at those options within the congregation's life cycle and its effect on shared assumptions. We then will approach the notion of marginality in a different way as we discuss the importance of seeking to be effective rather than to win.

ASSUMPTIONS AND THE LIFE CYCLE

In chapter 5, we introduced three phases through which a congregation passes if it survives across many years. We used the terms younger, established, and weakening to characterize primary features of each of these three phases of a church's life cycle. Conflict in a congregation is influenced by these phases; what is at stake in the conflict depends to a significant degree on the phase itself. Furthermore, since shared assumptions also affect the nature of conflict, their role in life cycle phases is critical to understand. Part of pastoral strategy in conflict, then, is to assess the interplay between the life cycle phase and the shared assumptions that are beginning to surface.

Younger phase. In this phase, the congregation is still trying out things, still growing, still learning. Conflicts between the pastor and the church in this phase often symbolize the need to learn something new, to handle a situation well, and thus to develop a strong, new shared assumption (which will join the others already in place). In other words, conflict stands for an opportunity for the church to make clear in its action what is important to it. "What shape will our vision take place? How will it play out?" These are key questions at stake within a conflict.

Pastors in younger-phase churches stand in a better position to influence the parish's shared assumptions. Assumptions are still being developed, since so many more aspects of its young life are still being negotiated, compared with churches in the later phases. This does not mean, however, that the pastor can "embed" whatever espoused values into assumptions that the pastor desires.[14] The congregation has to be willing to trust the pastor and discover in its own experience whether the pastor's ideas will work.[15]

If, for whatever reason, the members do not trust the pastor in a particular situation, they likely will resist the pastor's efforts. This will create conflict which, if handled poorly, will hurt the congregation. It will end up learning a pessimistic assumption instead of one that will serve them constructively later. One hopes that the pastor will recognize the importance of helping the parish come to resolution in a healthy way. This kind of outcome creates stronger assumptions, a stronger church culture, and greater potential for doing beneficial ministry together.

Established. Once a church has accomplished a number of things and feels secure about its future, it enters a different life cycle phase. Becoming established means having facilities and resources of which the membership is proud; it means being comfortable with what and who is familiar; it means being able to ride out unexpected incidents or developments; it involves often subtle networks that operate with their own subcultures within the congregation.[16] These subcultures share some assumptions in common, but each one has a few assumptions that are distinctly its own. Established churches are not very interested in, or able to, change; they enjoy having arrived at where they now live. They expect their pastors to fit in with their culture, rather than trying to change it.

What first challenges a pastor entering an established congregation is learning all the various subcultures, their quirks and contributions. An astute pastor comes to appreciate all this variety within the umbrella of the congregation. The challenge does not end with benign tolerance, however. Lurking below the surface of the established congregation's culture is an important question: "How will we live together?" In some churches, the music department gets what it wants more often than others. In other churches, it might be the education or mission groups. The pastor is in danger of siding with one group at the risk of not honoring the others. As seasoned pastors already know, this scenario is full of land mines!

A pastor who realizes that conflict is beginning to brew in the established church needs to step back and see what subcultural claims are competing with each other. Then she or he must, with great honesty, discern how he or she is being perceived in the midst of the competing claims. These two hard looks will provide the kind of insights that the pastor needs to proceed with a strategy that can benefit the congregation as a whole.

Weakening. Congregations that have become rigid, that are not interested in what occurs around them, that are less active and losing members (especially children/youth), and that operate by long-term member networks are in the weakening phase. Often, such a weakening condition sneaks up on a church ever so slowly, if its context seems stable and the old-timers seek the comfort of repetition. Early in this phase, a church can work through certain struggles, but, as the decline progresses, it becomes increasingly weaker.

Often at this point I have seen churches look for younger, energetic pastors who will attract new, younger people. Members espouse the value of growing with new blood, but all too often this value is undermined by a shared assumption that is contrary (e.g., "Only those of us who have been here for decades have any right to power"). The new pastor, hearing this espoused value and trusting its sincerity, then proceeds to reach out and add to the weak congregation's community. Yet, once new people begin to appear, their new ideas, practices, and interests are perceived as a threat to the old ways (long-standing shared assumptions). A confused and frustrated pastor often emerges out of such a scenario. She or he cannot understand the contradiction of the church's behavior: "They say one thing but do something else." By this time, conflict very likely has surfaced, and the pastor unfortunately becomes the easy victim, the scapegoat.

Deep inside the life of a weakening congregation lies a question that the old-timers do not want to be forced to ask. That question is, "How can we survive if we give in to this threat?" Few, if any, of the old-timers even would be conscious that this is what they fear. It is a different question from what congregations ask themselves in the other two phases. Hence, a pastor must use a different strategy to respond to it.

In such situations, one of the first key tactics is to recognize conflict just as it begins to surface. If they perceive a threat to their way of life, weakening congregations can be shockingly irrational. It would be foolish for their pastor to dismiss their displays of anxiety, even though the pastor should not be tempted to share in it. A declining church culture is rigid; it appears strong but is actually brittle. The assumptions that are old and cherished are beginning to show, and this will frighten longtime church members.

Pastors in these situations need to walk that sometimes fine line between anxiety at one extreme and apathy at the other. Being skilled in pastoral care will help to strengthen the trust that the pastor needs to help the congregation. Yet, if the pastor has been named as part of the problem, trust will be more difficult to gain. It will require on the part of the pastor some humility and strength of character to backtrack from a particular action or proposal and focus instead on the bigger picture.

A MEASURE OF MARGINALITY

All three of these basic pastoral strategies for conflict share one thing in common. No matter in what phase the pastor finds the church to be, one of his or her greatest challenges is in maintaining a degree of marginality toward the congregation. By marginality, we do not mean the common focus in current public discourse—the condition of certain groups of people who, because of racial, ethnic, educational, or economic factors are chronically pushed to the edge of society. These kinds of marginality clearly do exist, and surely the gospel has something to say about it.

For our purposes here, marginality refers to an attitude of relative emotional and cultural distance that a wise pastor maintains between herself or himself and the congregation.[17] In other words, pastors monitor themselves so as not to identify completely with the congregation that they are serving. They come to know a lot about the congregation's history and people; they come to love the people and support their needs; they preach, teach, and manage the parish's overall operations; and they do so effectively by maintaining an eagle's view on everything. Marginality is the counterpoint to the theme of chapter 2, where we discussed how pastors get adopted by their churches. Both adoption and marginality are necessary features of pastors who get along well with their churches.

Becoming marginal to your parish is neither automatic nor easy. Yet, when conflict appears on the horizon, it is most necessary. Even when conflict is not present, pastors need to learn how not to get absorbed by their role. This prestrategic perspective was discussed at some length in chapter 4. In order to be of good use to their congregations, pastors must discipline themselves to retain a measure of emotional and cultural distance. This is the only way to acquire enough perspective on the church to remain honest about what is going on.

For pastors who have not been at their posts long, or for itinerant pastors who rarely stay in one parish long, marginality almost comes with the territory. Yet conscientious pastors new on the job might try to compensate for or speed up their knowledge curve, hoping to prove themselves that much faster. This strategy easily could backfire, as the discussion of pastoral adoption in chapter 2 suggests. Marginality should not be viewed as bad. The nature and use of the marginality are more important. A pastor facing conflict needs to be able to step back and get a better view of what is actually taking place.

Sometimes this function can be performed helpfully with the aid of a trusted person outside the congregation. He or she is neither enmeshed in the church's day-to-day matters nor invested in any particular plans or outcomes. Having such a sounding board can help a pastor in "warm water" to see things that, by being close to the action, otherwise might be shielded. The pastor not only begins to see the situation more fully, but also learns to understand himself or herself better. Weak, insecure pastors do not help their churches when conflict rears its ugly head. If you are not sure who you are, you certainly are not capable of helping the congregation understand itself, especially when the two of you are at odds.

BEING "RIGHT" OR EFFECTIVE

More than most other professions (except perhaps politicians!), pastors are susceptible to notions of grandiosity. We enter pastoral ministry with intentions of helping people by bringing the gospel to bear on their lives. Few other forms of lifework call for such a degree of commitment to high ideals. However, it is tempting for pastors to believe that the ideals are the only things that matter. We can suppose that every gap between what we perceive the ideals to be and the realities that face us must be ardently and immediately overcome. This level of zeal seduces us sometimes into believing that the most important thing for a pastor is being "right."

Being "right" in a conflict might not help your church. It does not take much for the zealous pastor seeking to be right to move into self-righteousness. Then conflict becomes a standoff or, worse, a power struggle. Conflict that escalates to this point usually ends up damaging the congregation, whether the pastor feels set back by the situation or not. The parish with a bad experience of conflict learns shared assumptions that revolve around protection rather than healthy adventure.

Remember the incarnation. Pastors who are too concerned about being right often have a theological problem: They do not yet understand the meaning of incarnation. Our Christian faith asserts that God has come to dwell among us, "Immanuel." This divine initiative is what makes grace possible. We do not follow God because we can earn God's favor but because God has been unbelievably good to us. How do we know? Our best evidence is in Jesus the Messiah, "God with us."

If we pastors start to feel that we have to dig in our heels when the congregation is resisting us, perhaps we need another dose of incarnational theology. That dose can help restore the larger view of what the congregation needs, rather than which doctrine about our authority that we are trying to uphold. That dose can help us assess how much cultural capital we can afford to lose in the situation. If Jesus was willing to die for the sins of the world, then surely we can die to our pastoral egos and high-and-mighty convictions enough to try to help the congregation. The congregation needs to heal from negative experiences, present and past. It needs to embrace more of the life around it. It needs to learn how to learn about both faith and witness. It needs to change things, if it is going to respond to changes around it. Paying attention to congregational needs like these is what helps make a pastor effective. Let being right take care of itself.

GOING AGAINST THE GRAIN

If there is anywhere that the church could show the world that it marches to a different drummer, it just might be in the way that it handles conflict. Understanding the cultural dynamics of church conflicts provides a way to establish our community experience over the competitive, superficial behaviors of our American macroculture. There is a deep sense in which being Christian calls for being different—not just as individuals but also in our fellowship. Seeing the deeper, cultural factors at work in our conflicts affords us a creative window for replacing "win-lose" with something more blessed. We can stop either jumping quickly to blame or maneuvering power plays. Instead, we can seek to incarnate the gospel within our struggle. There are no easy ways to do this, but the discussion of this chapter does identify a number of basic insights and strategies. Utilizing these, incarnation becomes something that we live out in such a way that it transforms. It will make us different, as persons and as a fellowship. From there, it can stimulate transformation in the world in which we live. So a lot is at stake when we start to fight! Let's not destroy our chance to keep on witnessing to our faith.

Anyone who has been through a church conflict knows that it triggers a concern for power. This chapter helps us realize that power is always played out in the context of a particular culture. Churches are affected by these same dynamics of conflict and power as any other human group. Yet, as we have just seen, our Christian calling holds out a countercultural way of working through difference. This countercultural way is grounded in the incarnation.

The apostle Paul interpreted Jesus' life and purpose many times, with many stimulating images. In Philippians 2, he recites what appears to be an early hymn as he speaks of the practical need for churches to live in unity and humility. The hymn says that Jesus did not count equality with God as something to which he clung tightly, "to be exploited" (2:6). Rather, he "emptied himself " (2:7), becoming human, becoming as a slave. It was that drastic obedience to God that led to his crucifixion, the lowest, most despicable form of death in the ancient Roman world.

This image of Jesus, the incarnate One who dies on a cross, is one that pastors easily forget when discord appears. We don't like to be humiliated and have power grabbed away from us, do we? Yet I would venture to guess that pastors following the model of Jesus from Philippians 2 would do wonders for churches. I do not mean rolling over and playing dead, but giving up the need to control and look good. As we begin to understand the cultural dynamics of our church, we are less likely to get caught up in dissension in adversarial terms. We will be more equipped to find constructive ways to work through things. We will be incarnating the gospel in ways that perhaps the parish has not witnessed before.

Rev. Tennyson, the pastor who had submitted his letter of resignation to his church, did not leave. The council, having listened to testimony from many members and conversations, decided that their congregation needed this pastor who strove to raise their level of faith and witness. The vote to reject his resignation was unanimous. A resolution was signed, supporting the good pastor's vision of the church's continued involvement in the community. And so Rev. Tennyson remained as pastor of St. Matthew Church—for another twenty-one years.

It would be foolish to suppose that discord between pastor and parish is easy to solve or will be free of harm. Yet, it would be equally foolish to think that the only way to manage conflict is to give up on Christian charity and slug it out. Seeking out the cultural symbolism of church conflict offers a powerful way to approach the various deeper needs creatively and redemptively. It is my prayer that you will prepare yourself to treat your church conflict in new ways because you now better understand the cultural capital that is involved in it.

Saying Goodbye

When Is It Time to Move On?

HOW DO YOU KNOW?

Years ago, I met Pastor Wagner in the town to which I had just moved. In his seventh year as pastor of one of the local Baptist churches, Pastor Wagner was quiet but friendly, young but overweight and treating a heart condition, and devoted to his wife and three young children. He was conscientious in his duties but privately shared that he had his moments. Once I had told him something about the frustration that I was feeling about my new call. Then he confided in me: "When I first came to this church, I could not tell if people liked me or not or if they thought that I was doing a good job or not. There were days when I felt so discouraged about my ministry here, if the owner of the grocery store down the street had offered me a job as a box boy, I would have taken it."

A few years later, another colleague in a different setting told me about a pastor he had met at a conference. This young man had graduated from seminary barely four years earlier. He had asked my friend for some help with his dossier, since he had decided to change churches. However, it was not his first move as a pastor, neither his second. This young pastor, in just his fourth year after ordination, already was seeking his fourth church call!

Compare this "jackrabbit" pastor to that of Rev. Bruce (from chapter 3), a Methodist pastor assigned to a small, younger parish in a rural area. The church was barely thirty years old but when Rev. Bruce arrived, he discovered it to be lethargic, guarded, and suspicious of outsiders. Rev. Bruce realized that something must have happened in its brief history to have created among the membership such low morale. Instead of prying, however, the sensitive pastor began to get to know the members. He smiled a lot, affirmed each person, listened to their stories, attended special events, preached about love, grace, gifts for ministry, and the like. As time went by, a few members began to open up to the devoted pastor about the church's gloomy past. The stories that they shared explained to Rev. Bruce why they displayed so little energy. After five years as their pastor, he sensed that the parish was strong enough to start looking at its own future. But would he be able to stay long enough to help them? Would the bishop understand what he was trying to do and allow him further time to strengthen this fragile congregation?

WHEN DO WE SAY GOODBYE?

One of the more delicate challenges of pastoral ministry emerges whenever we pastors are getting ready to leave one church for another. Although some pastors stay with their congregations for a lifetime, the vast majority of pastors who serve many years will do so in more than one congregation.[1] Methodists and others who are appointed in itinerant ministries regularly face comings and goings in churches. Yet, in spite of this common pastoral phenomenon, most of us who move around do not have a very good idea about how to handle the process. We might try to be holy or theological as we justify our specific decisions, but if we are honest, sometimes it feels almost like a crapshoot.

Getting along with your church includes gracious leave-taking. For pastors in call positions, leave-taking is tied up in the particular reasons that you are going, the timing itself, and the way that you say goodbye. For pastors in appointments, leave-taking occurs regularly and is affected by the sometimes-sudden polity of itineration. Either way that pastors come and go, we can be more authentically effective if we conceive of the process in terms of culture.

In this chapter, we will look at the matter of "when the pastor leaves." Because the actual decision for leave-taking varies depending on call or appointment traditions, we thus will treat the question as having two elements. One is, How does a pastor with the freedom to leave a church discern when that time has come? The other is, When you know that you are leaving (whether for a new call or a new appointment), how can you design the leave-taking in such a way that the church will be more able to move on? Answers to these questions will be shaped by the framework informed by cultural capital. The ways in which this capital is available and at work in your scenario shapes your parting opportunity to serve your congregation.

BIBLICAL LEAVE-TAKING

When we survey in the Scriptures the many situations in which God's leaders take leave, we find little that equates closely with today's typical pastoral movement. In the Hebrew Bible, when God told Abram and Sarai to leave their home and journey to a land they would be shown (Gen. 12:1), they were not given a map or a deadline. Joshua succeeded Moses with the latter's laying on of hands, having been selected by God for the task (Num. 27:12–23; compare Deut. 34:9). Elisha succeeded the renowned Elijah (2 Kings 2), after asking for a double portion of the powerful prophet's spirit (v. 9) and then watching him disappear up into the sky (v. 11). The kings of Israel and Judah succeeded each other by death, sometimes through stealth. None of these stories and reports provides very authoritative guidelines for pastoral departures.

New Testament evidence is no more decisive. Jesus carried on an itinerant ministry, having selected twelve men as his inner circle, along with a larger, mixed following of disciples. Jesus' ministry did not last long, though, ending in what we would have to call a unique way. Following his resurrection, Jesus imparted the Holy Spirit to his followers (John 20:22; Acts 2:1–5) and sent out the twelve to spread the good news (Matt. 28:16–20). Not too many years later, the apostle Paul was busy with his own, much wider, itinerant ministry. Yet he also gave no directions concerning pastoral transitions and saying goodbye. Perhaps the early conditions of the Jesus movement had not created the need to address such issues.

So, beyond the usual biblical platitudes about being loving and decent to one another, where do pastors turn to receive insight about closing the circle of their ministry in one place? In order to discover some useful and beneficial answers, we first will consider some general features that influence our understanding and practice of pastoral movement.

THE PASTORAL "CAREER" TODAY

There are a few basic elements of life today that deeply affect how pastors view what they do. One of them can be described with the metaphor of the corporate ladder. Another one results from changes in demographic patterns.

CORPORATE LADDER

As was suggested in the previous chapter, many aspects of our church life have been influenced heavily by values and practices reflected in the dominant form of organization of the twentieth century, the business corporation. These values and practices have shaped the ways that clergy in many denominations perceive and exercise ministry. I remember as a young pastor becoming aware of new pastors like myself who were on the "fast track." They dressed the right way, talked the right way, knew and met all the right people, and already were on the staffs of large churches. Some of them struck me as being no more gifted than I thought I was. Yet they seemed more prepared and eager to make their way up the church's "corporate ladder" (however it was perceived).

I also came to notice various ways that the older, more experienced, pastors behaved toward one another in terms of attention, deference, and respect. What gradually became apparent to me in those early years as a pastor was a set of assumptions about pastoral career. The messages that I gleaned from these early observations usually were unspoken or alluded to in obtuse ways. Yet they left strong impressions on me. Some of them are as follows:

- Talented young pastors had "ambition."
- Small churches were stepping-stones to larger ones.

- Rural churches were to be avoided if at all possible.
- The first couple of pastoral positions would be shorter in duration than the later, more desirable ones.
- Compensation packages would be commensurately larger with each new, desired move.
- A pastor's status within the denomination and community would increase over time.
- Pastors who stayed "too long" in smaller churches were not very good pastors, especially if they were over forty-five years old.
- Getting known and liked by denominational officials increased one's chances of enhancing one's pastoral career.
- In any particular region, only a handful of your denomination's congregations were the most desirable to serve.

As I look back now, I interpret these ideas as shared assumptions that were alive and well within seminaries and denominational structures. My point in mentioning them here is not so much to critique or condemn them as it is to bring insight to bear on what influences pastors to stay or go.

Taken as a whole, though, I do believe that this set of assumptions does reflect more of a business model of work than it does service in pastoral ministry. This contrast, while not an absolute one (and I certainly do not want to be naively uncritical about the comparisons), does help us become aware of our churches' setting in macroculture. The fish tank of American society is a difficult one from which any one school of fish might seek to extract itself. We need, therefore, to make ourselves more aware of such macrocultural assumptions, for we might be operating by many of them without question.

DEMOGRAPHICS OF THE PASTOR

Until recently, persons who answered the call to pastoral ministry typically did so early in life. This meant that they would complete their apprenticeships or theological training while still young and then serve for forty or fifty years. Since the 1970s, however, the average age of seminarians has increased. Seminary recruiters will tell you that it is no longer typical for the new seminary student to be twenty-two or twenty-three years old. Instead, that person is over thirty, forty, and sometimes even fifty—and just as often as not a woman. Many of these people enter seminary after careers in business, education, law, and so forth. Seminary graduates today thus have less years of life left in which to engage in pastoral work.

Whether this trend will continue indefinitely or not remains to be seen. However, for the foreseeable future, it means that more and more churches are seeing pastors whose "careers" read differently from those of new batches of graduates twenty-five years ago. Pastors are more likely to have run a business, raised children at home, left an accomplished practice, or had other significant life experiences prior to having become a pastor. These pastors in many respects are more mature, more broadly experienced, but less technically savvy as a pastor for someone their age. They often have a stronger sense of what ministry means to them. Some of them made significant sacrifices to follow this call. For many of them, issues of status, power, and security are less important.

"KNOW THYSELF"

As a pastor, where do you find yourself within this complex mix of business models and demographic shifts? What does "serving the church" mean to you? How do you reconcile service in a society that believes "bigger is better"? How do you feel among a gathering of your colleagues, knowing something about the differences in your incomes and status? How do laypeople treat you in your current position? What is important to you right now, if you thought about leaving?

POWER TO THE PEOPLE

A pastor's coming or going also affects the dynamics within the parish itself. Departures trigger, at least to some degree, a pending change among the activity and influence of particular members. Certain pastors will appeal more to certain members than to others; these understandable realities can and do affect which members participate in which of the church's activities. Since this dynamic of preference cannot be anticipated in its details, some members in your parish could feel threatened by a pending pastoral change. Others might welcome it as an opportunity to promote pet projects that have not yet received as much attention as they would like.

Such effects on the congregation, however, are not simply due to members' individual preferences; they also are modulated by the denomination's polity. As our earlier discussion already has implied, pastoral departures in call traditions differ from those in appointment traditions. Let us look briefly at these two polities, in terms of how the churches might be likely to respond to the pastor's leaving.

APPOINTMENTS

Methodist and other Wesleyan parishes, by necessity, become accustomed to living with the reality that their pastor's tenure depends on other factors besides their own preference. Methodist pastors agree to itinerate, to move from parish to parish as the bishop sees fit. The cultures of these congregations, therefore, share some similar assumptions about the role of their pastors. Their experience tells them that pastors do not normally stay long enough to leave too decisive of a mark on the parish's culture.

When appointed pastors then are moved to another charge, the church often not only misses them dearly but also knows that "this is the way it is with us." The congregation learns to rely on itself over the long haul, since pastors come and go. Practically speaking, this means that longtime church members, rather than the pastor, tend to have more sway in appointment-system parishes than their pastors do. Those members who feel that they have the most to lose in a change are most likely to try to maintain what they think they have. A newly appointed pastor is less able to overcome the cultural capital of longtime church members.

CALLS

Churches who call their pastors sometimes have a more difficult time seeing them leave. Calls most often are open-ended, with no time limit set for the duration of the pastor's stay. In some traditions, as we have seen,

pastors are expected to stay many years, and if they founded the congregation, they very well could end up "dying in the saddle" of that pulpit. Many
other call traditions see their pastors serve several churches over the years.
Called pastors tend to stay longer in one place. Longer tenure increases the
likelihood of those pastors becoming more fully adopted by the congregation and more fully part of its culture. The more closely that the pastor is
identified with the church's culture, the greater the chance of disrupting
the cultural balance in the church when the pastor leaves.

These distinctions of influence between called and appointed pastors
are generalizations that, of course, do not apply in every single parish situation. Distinctions they are, nonetheless, for they do identify broad ten-
dencies. They help us appreciate more fully how a congregation's culture is
symbolized. The way in which a pastor takes leave of a church becomes
part of the story of her or his legacy. One would hope that we pastors will
be concerned to leave a legacy that will bless the church, not simply promote ourselves.

LIFE CYCLE PHASES AND PASTORAL DEPARTURE

Yet there is even more that can be said about the cultural dimensions of
pastoral leave-taking. Remember that every congregation's culture is
deeply influenced by its life cycle phase. For purposes of simplicity, in
this book we have categorized church life cycles into three phases: younger,
growing; established; and weakening.[2] The primary characteristics of these
three phases help pastors identify the kinds of questions to ask themselves as they decide whether to move on or as they anticipate a new appointment.

YOUNG AND GROWING

Younger-phase congregations are characterized mainly by being flexible.
Charter members still abound and are active. Customs and traditions still
are taking shape. Resources are still a challenge to develop and keep. These
kinds of churches literally depend for their success on the commitments

and contributions of a few key people. Pastors who found a church or who agree to do a "new church start" for their denomination are among those key persons.

For the sake of simplicity and clarity (which sometimes are elusive qualities in the parish!), let us assume for the moment that such a younger church in question has been negotiating all of its challenges fairly well. Not everyone who has "checked out the church" has stayed, but neither have any disagreements led to a split. If you are the pastor of such a congregation and are contemplating whether to continue there, ask yourself honestly about the contributions that you have made to this neophyte community of faith:

• *How well have you taught them to solve problems?* Sometimes members of new congregations want so much for things to turn out well all the time that they harbor unrealistic expectations. Challenges and difficulties abound for the new church. It is in the nature of things that some of what a church has to decide or do will be troubling. You do not want this young church to grow up naive! Our Christian faith declares trust in a God who is in our midst in spite of what happens. The God of scripture is the wondrous opportunist, who unflaggingly works to bring redemption and wholeness. Surely we can learn to see that kind of God involved in all the hassles and quandaries that present themselves to a young church!

• *What have you done to promote the creation of strong, positive shared assumptions?* This question is closely tied to the first one. We have been speaking in this book of an interpretive framework for churches that take very seriously the presence and power of culture. At its most basic, culture consists of shared, basic assumptions that a group or community forms in response to testing out values in their experience. One central task for younger churches is to discover what works. Pastors in churches that are still shaping many of their assumptions have a responsibility to help those shaping experiences be constructive.

In other words, pastors of churches in this first phase of organizational life are in a key position to strengthen the congregation for the long haul. It needs to learn such assumptions as:

"We can control what we do well enough to accomplish things."

"Our faith in God will sustain us, even in hard times."

"We can trust each other."

If a pastor is confident that the church is discovering these kinds of assumptions to be true, she or he is doing something that is both right and effective. Churches like this are more likely to handle the transition from one pastor to another in a healthy way.

• *Is the church developing team ministry?* One notion about Christian life and witness that has gained prominence in the last couple of decades is that of working together. This might sound odd to say, as though it were self-evident. A look around parishes today, however, would suggest that authentic sharing of power, responsibility, and activity are not as common as we might suppose. Young, formative churches that become strong are ones that are grounded in some measure of group undertaking. Pastors who create a church that depends too much on the pastor have done the congregation a disservice. Yes, the pastor in a young church must be strong, focused, and inspiring. But not every style "from the top" will help a church deal with changes along the way.

It is especially crucial for the long-term health and vitality of a congregation that it learns in its young phase to function as a team. In my opinion, the greatest compliment that a pastor ever could be paid would come in a situation that the following story reveals. A busy, growing church hired a consultant to help them make some decisions about significant new opportunities. On the appointed day and time, the consultant arrived at the church building. There he was introduced to nine members of the church's staff, by name only—no titles were used. Then he joined the staff in its weekly meeting. It was an animated, energetic, respectful experience; everyone had a chance to be heard and to share ideas. The consultant listened and observed carefully. Finally, after an hour or so, he interrupted their cordial and productive proceedings: "Excuse me, I am very impressed with your meeting, but I just want to ask one question at this point: Which one of you is the pastor?"

Here was a congregation whose pastor knew how to be a team player. When time came for him or her to move on, this congregation would be much stronger for their many successful experiences of working together. If you have helped your church work as a team, then you can leave with some confidence of a job well done.

ESTABLISHED

In the middle phase of a church's life cycle, the congregation is confident in its continuity. It can survive, even if for a time it is not that interested in adapting to changes. Established congregations have more than one sub-culture, based on the various activities and networks that have developed over the years (including family/clan-based associations). As we noted in chapter 6, these subcultures represent the particular interests, agendas, and values of the several elements of the parish's life. Subcultures do not always see eye to eye. One challenge in the established church, then, is to maintain commitment to something in common that is worthy of the parish's time and energy.

Pastors who might be leaving their service to an established congregation would do well to consider the following issues. Each issue is concerned with the church's ability to:

- *Focus on its common vision.* The pastor needs to have helped the congregation identify and enthusiastically affirm a direction into God's future that unifies, not divides, it. A parish will not be healthy if the various groups are more interested in what they are doing than in how what they do contributes to the church's mission overall. Pastors need to move beyond simply negotiating peaceful coexistence between these various groups. Rather, his or her job is to assist the church's mutual purpose in remaining paramount.

  This is not an easy task, but it needs doing. One established but weakening church had a long tradition of classic Western-style music performance excellence. For years, the congregation had been willing to pay section leaders and a highly skilled organist in order to maintain this aspect of the congregation's life. As time went by, however, younger adults joined the church, parents who appreciated the music but saw other needs being sacrificed. Some of these parents questioned the size of the music budget in light of waning attention to education and youth ministry.

The parish's music department responded by designing and administering a congregational survey. Once the results had been tabulated, the department, somewhat triumphfulistically, announced that the survey indicated strong support for continuing the music program as it was. High favorable percentages to the questions were quoted. Yet the survey itself was flawed. The group who had the most to lose from an unfavorable response put it together. The questions were worded in such a way that even the young parents who criticized the music budget ended up answering most questions favorably. No other church programs or activities were included in the survey. No questions about the church's mission, or the music department's role in helping fulfill that mission, were asked.

This survey thus reinforced the existing agenda of that congregation's music subculture. It stifled any opportunity for a deeper discussion about where the church was headed. It hamstrung any further effort to help church officials bridge gaps between the congregation's subcultures. Pastors who are good for established parishes have worked at helping the various groups talk with one another, take on common tasks, and look at the future together.

- *Balance continuity with new opportunity.* One danger in the established life cycle phase is becoming so rigid that the church loses its ability to adapt. No congregation can survive indefinitely if it simply clings to its traditions. Eventually, changes in the world around it will force the congregation itself to change or gradually die (more on this concern below). A pastor helping an established church has supported efforts to try some new things, to blend some new elements into the familiar ones.

- *Learn how to learn.* Established congregations possess a set of shared assumptions that worked well for them in their formative phase. As time goes by, however, some of the conditions under which certain assumptions emerged are no longer valid. A recession hits the community; war calls soldiers away and creates hardships stateside; the neighborhood residents are aging and beginning to be replaced by families of a different ethnic group; a social movement (e.g., the Great Awakening, civil rights) elevates certain values to fresh prominence; and so forth. One of the most important assumptions that a church can learn in its formative phase is that it knows how to learn new things. If an established congregation did not learn about learning when it was young, the challenge to learn later will be perceived as unnecessary. This perception, if not changed, eventually harms the church.

Pastors who might be leaving their established churches should ask themselves how they have helped their churches face new circumstances. Are they simply repeating what they have done before? If so, what can you do to encourage them to see new things as openings for continued growth? What will your leave-taking symbolize to the present culture?

WEAKENING

Shrinking activity, vague vision, strong cliques, preoccupation with form: These four characteristics dominate congregations in the weakening life cycle phase. Concern for the future occasionally breaks out into irrational diversionary incidents over membership, upkeep of facilities, programs, and youth. Sometimes pastors who first arrive at a declining church are aware of its weakened condition. Often, however, the seriousness of its rigid way of life becomes evident only in the pastor's day-to-day parish interactions. Called pastors might have taken the call in order to turn the church around. Appointed pastors might be tempted to ride out the low-energy charge and hope for a better appointment later. On the other hand, they might seek to spark renewal, hoping that they are reappointed for enough years to see results.

Pastors in weakening churches who want to assess the value of their tenure there can ask themselves the following questions:

- *How well has this church come to grips with its current situation?* Until a weakening church pulls its head out of the sand and looks around its landscape, it has little hope for the future. Pastors need to avoid both extreme strategies—on the one hand, of placating the church without drawing it into a sober self-assessment, or, on the other hand, of ridiculing the church, hoping to shame it into action. Instead, the effective pastor will find a fitting way to engage the church's key culture-bearers in truth telling, about itself and its setting.

- *Have I provided assurance in the face of uncertainty?* Declining churches are weakening because they have not learned how to learn—or else the memories of their first-generation learning have been lost. Part of the paralysis of decline exhibits itself when longtime church members finally realize that something is wrong, but they cannot imagine what to do about it.

  Pastors who are leading weakening churches skillfully offer a word of realistic hope at this point. Some of the most dramatic stories from the Bible tell of moments when God's people thought that all was lost. Within the declining congregation, many of these scriptural accounts have lost their power. Bible studies and sermons that deal with God "making a way out of no way" are, for a declining church, most appropriate, as well as being deeply theological.

- *What kind of a glimpse have I provided them of a new vision from God?* Declining churches not only need to know that there is hope, but they also need some idea of what that hope might look like. It probably is not a good idea for a pastor of a declining church to trot out his or her own full-blown version of a new vision. Instead, holding up potential elements of such a vision stands a better chance of being well received. The congregation has to embrace any new vision, and this means that the old one—and its shared assumptions—will be at least substantially modified. Culture is at stake here, and being the conserving mechanism that it is, culture does not change quickly or easily.

  Let us spell out the implications of this insight in a little more detail. A new vision for a declining congregation will comprise a mixture of old values and shared assumptions and some espoused values that have not been internalized (i.e., turned into assumptions). If the longtime members of the parish can see how the pursuit of some new values can be blended with some of the former "tried-and-true" assumptions, they will be likely to resist less. They also will feel less anxiety, because they can see the picture of the vision more clearly this way. In many cases, the new vision does not need to be "completely different" from the former one. A skilled pastor knows how to connect the new vision with familiar values and assumptions.

- *How many substantial steps has this congregation taken toward that new vision?* A pastor who gets a weakening church excited about a new future but is not there to help them start following it does that parish more harm than good. Remember, it takes time and some focused energy for a declining church to move from mere willingness to successful action. The weight of the past will be strong.

  The church's membership, especially the key bearers of its dominant (but declining) culture, needs to test this new combination of values and assumptions and in specific ways. Pastors who lead in these situations will help the church decide where to begin trying out their new vision. The pastor will encourage but not demand, suggest but not require, participate but not dominate. Eventually, the vision will need to be heavily symbolized in weekly worship, but worship might not be the place to put the main energy at first.

The purpose of the sets of questions listed above is to help you as pastor evaluate the impact of your ministry. Questions like these allow you to be more discerning about the contributions that you have made to the parish in question. Such honest assessment focuses, not as a narcissistic review, but rather on what has been accomplished in and by the congregation. From here, you will have a better idea of what you would be leaving if you were no longer their pastor.

THE CULTURAL CAPITAL OF DEPARTURE

With this model of assessment before us, let us look for a few moments at pastoral leave-taking specifically in terms of cultural capital. These comments will draw the theme to a close before we discuss some final practical advice for calls and for appointments.

HOW MANY CHIPS DO YOU HAVE?

Our discussion from the previous section presupposes that the pastors undertaking any of the suggested strategies already would have the necessary cultural capital to be effective. Given these terms, one general question for the pastor contemplating departure to ask is, "What cultural capital do I have at my disposal in this parish?" This question will lead the reflective pastor through all the themes that we have discussed in this book up to now: knowing what you are getting into; becoming adopted by the parish; turning busy-ness into ministry; carrying bad news; becoming a leader; and dealing with conflict. Each one of these themes represents potential development and/or use of a pastor's cultural capital within a church.

It is hoped that you will have at least some of this kind of capital to use as you leave. It is too late when you are receiving a new appointment to ask yourself how well your adoption went at your present parish! This is why it is so important for pastors to think about their cultural capital as soon as they know which church they will be serving next. Yet, as we have observed already, the purpose of such anticipation and appraisal is not for the pastor's own glorification. If we are truly going to serve that parish, our constant question must be, "How is my being here benefiting this church?"

PREPARING THE WAY

One way to make your eventual leave-taking easier is to institute an annual conversation on the state of the church with its elected officials. As pastor, you will be better prepared by having reflected on the appropriate questions for your church's phases ahead of time. Then, design the review process with the board's president or clerk. Remember that the perspective from each phase of the church's life cycle will be different, so your questions and process have to be adjusted accordingly. You cannot expect complete awareness and honesty from the board, especially the first time. These officers are not so much trying to deceive you or withhold information as they more likely are not going to be very aware of their church's cultural depths.

Neither is this conversation a soapbox opportunity for you, the pastor. Unless the board has grossly neglected its duty in some flagrant way, annual conversation is not a place for the pastor to scold or berate. Even if it were necessary strategically, your cultural capital will be played better by discussing your concerns privately first with a trusted board member. The tone of this conversation should be steeped in celebration. Like our biblical ancestors, we believers today need from time to time to remind ourselves of what God has been doing in our midst. Too easily, it all is taken for granted. Use your role as their resident pastoral theologian to ask leading questions such as, "How have you seen God active in our accomplishments this year?" Discussion flowing from a question like this can help church officers affirm church activity, strengthen theological insight, inspire spiritual growth, and stimulate commitment to vision.

THE NEED FOR RITUAL AND CEREMONY

A congregation that is accustomed to periodic self-assessment is better prepared to say "goodbye" when a pastor leaves. You can help them maximize their blessings by attending to the ways in which the departure can be fittingly ritualized and ceremonialized. Rituals—one-on-one or in very small groups—can occur both formally and casually; ceremonies are public and formal (in the sense that they are planned out, liturgized ahead of time). Ask yourself, "How do I say goodbye to each constituency in this parish?" There are key laypersons with whom you have labored, staff members, organizations, and auxiliaries (boards, women's groups, etc.), sick and shut-ins whom you have visited, and so on. There is Sunday worship, in which your final Sunday shall be filled with symbols of closure. Depending on the amount of time available, you will attend lunches, dinners, and parties; you will call on a few persons, some of whom are important to the congregation and some just to you. Your final words will be of accomplishment ("See what God has done in our midst!"), affirmation ("You continue to be God's people"), and anticipation ("Behold, God is making all things new").

In other words, pay as much attention and energy to your leaving as you did to your laboring. If you help the congregation experience a blessed departure, chances are that it will be good for you, too. The ideas in this chapter will help you find plenty of latitude for leave-taking with honor and blessing. We pastors can avoid the extremes of leaving without a goodbye or of leaving like a diva! Knowing the dynamics of cultural capital could make all the difference—to you and certainly to the congregation.

FINAL WORDS ABOUT FINAL WORDS

Let us pull together a few loose ends on this often neglected subject of pastoral departure. Pastors often move more than once during their years of pastoral service. Attention to the cultural dynamics of congregations provides an invaluable lens for the peripatetic pastor, whether called or appointed. Learning to "read" the congregation's culture opens the pastor to many deep insights and helps identify appropriate strategies and tactics. When a culturally astute pastor is ready to move, both pastor and congregation are better equipped to celebrate and embrace their new opportunities.

ALL PASTORS

A pastor's overarching goal is to help the congregation maintain a strong and vital witness to its faith. One way that culture theory benefits pastors is by showing them why and how they can adjust their strategies and tactics. Not every church is in the same life cycle phase or has the same set of basic, shared assumptions. If a pastor approaches ministry as a "one-trick pony," she or he is not well equipped to serve many churches. It is possible for a motivated pastor to learn to use skills that are less interesting to them or well developed. The questions on the pastor's mind always must be, "What are the opportunities for doing ministry here, and what must I do to help them happen?"

Pastors also can learn not to get "move-happy." It could become tempting to suppose that, if things do not work out well in one church, you can just keep moving on. Certainly, not every call or appointment will turn out to be as rewarding as others. Yet it is important for pastors to learn from their experiences, not to avoid difficult situations just because they are difficult. There are things to learn about pastoral ministry from every situation, things that can increase the pastor's cultural acuity. Pastors do not have to be "perfect" before their congregation says goodbye with sincere thanks.

APPOINTED PASTORS

Itinerant pastors normally are members of a district or conference for life. Covering particular geographical areas, conferences develop their own idiosyncratic confluences of culture. Many, if not most, of them cover the wide range of population density that now characterizes North American life. Any one conference is likely to include charges that are rural and charges that are urban, parishes that are tiny and some that are quite large. Because of the polity of appointment traditions, the clergy in the specific conference are the ones who "cover the territory" of all those parishes over the years.

Therefore, it behooves appointed pastors to become quick studies. They need to learn how to read a parish promptly—to begin associating espoused values with particular artifacts, to start deciphering shared assumptions, to honor the parish's existing culture, to be a cooperative partner in the dance of adoption. As we saw in chapter 2, a pastor's assimilation experience into the congregation is crucial to his or her opportunities for ministry. That early experience enculturates the pastor, setting the (often unconscious) parameters in which she or he will function. When it is time for the pastor to move to another charge, the cultural capital accrued through the enculturation process is what the pastor has to invest during leave-taking.

One way that appointed pastors can prepare the parish for pastoral transitions is by establishing the custom of an annual assessment of the state of the church. Holding this gathering about a month or two before appointments are announced could provide a stimulus of reflection and expectation into which the parish needs to move during its next year. The manner in which such an event is organized and undertaken must be designed to be effective within that parish's idiosyncratic culture. Oral culture churches should not use "management by objective" techniques, for instance; these do not fit their way of life and will not be perceived as helpful or necessary.[3]

What is most important, no matter how formally or informally the assessment occurs, is that the church officers and staff talk over the year, listen to one another, and arrive at some common understandings of the church's present position. Through a regular experience like this, parish and pastor can bring at least some degree of closure to the current year. Then, if the pastor is moved, pastor and parish have a stronger foundation on which the leave-taking can be carried out.

It is hoped that appointed pastors also carry on regular conversations about their charges with their presiding elders or district superintendents. The context of such discussions centers on the continued suitability of the current match: How well is ministry taking place through this particular partnership between pastor and parish? Questions such as the following help to guide the sharing:

- In what ways is the congregation growing?
- What needs does it have, and which needs does it recognize?
- What do you as their pastor continue to offer to them?

As long as the conference official is persuaded that you can help this parish strengthen its ministry, you stand a better chance of remaining another year. If your ministry has been beneficial so far, another year most likely will aid the church even further.

Every appointed pastor realizes the limits on long-term effectiveness that itinerancy creates. We have explored in previous chapters some of these limits and do not want to diminish their realities here. In some appointment-tradition churches, the congregation has come to expect or desire less from their pastors than we might hope. If a pastor is going to stay a short time, say three to five years, what can she or he expect to be able to accomplish? On what will they be able to look back and hear a voice say, "Well done!" in spite of what the parish might have felt?

In a limited-time situation, pastors can still help their churches. Sometimes the best that you can hope for is to plow, plant, and water. *At the least, you can create conditions in which the parish is better able to name the truth about itself.* I do not mean that the pastor becomes confrontational, annoyingly prophetic, or distant. Rather, creating conditions involves an artful, flexible strategy that opens opportunities for church members and groups to be in an honest position to say, "This is who we are (warts and all)." You as pastor are not naming it for them; you are helping them to name it for themselves.

Congregations who can say who and where they are stand a much better chance of doing something positive. If some of its shared assumptions are old and not serving it well anymore, admitting as much lets the church become proactive. A proactive church then can begin to learn what it needs to learn. A key in this entire process is a pastor who is less interested in being right than in being effective.

CALLED PASTORS

Much of the advice for appointed pastors can be easily adapted for pastors in called positions. The main difference is that calls are open-ended. If a pastor is not forced out, she or he technically has the option of remaining for an indefinite time. So how does a called pastor know when it is time to move on?

This question is especially difficult for pastors who have founded congregations. The expectation might be that he or she will remain until death, but will that help the church in the long run? Perhaps your tradition allows you the freedom to establish a dynasty, to pass on the pastorate to a relative or someone else of your choosing. Will grooming someone to be "just like you" keep the church strong? Strictly speaking, probably not. The vision and skills that you as founding pastor bring to the growing congregation will not serve it well once it begins to settle in beyond survival.[4]

The challenge for any called pastor, then, is to stay fresh. Again, the focus should be on serving your call. What does the congregation need right now, in order to either attain, sustain, or regain a strong vision? If you can see clearly to answer this question, or find key members who will answer it, then you can decide if the task is for you. Why should you stay? What do you need as a pastor in order to feel fulfilled?

Most denominations using calls have structures and staff positions designed to help pastors. How might they assist you in evaluating the church and yourself? Who knows you well enough to help you see things about your present circumstances that you might not see? Perhaps even more importantly, what skills does your church call for right now that you have not developed well and could do so? Any time that we can learn to do more, we are increasing our ability to develop cultural capital wherever we go.

VOICE OF THE SPIRIT

Nothing that I have written here should be perceived as a substitute for making pastoral decisions spiritually. However, I have been concerned for years that what is labeled as "spiritual" somehow becomes disconnected from other ways in which we can know. I would hope that you would use everything in this book as partners to discernment. We human beings are not spiritual and intellectual and emotional and physical and social, as though each one of these elements could be excised from the others. Rather, all aspects of being human are intricately connected to the others.[5] The spiritual dimension of our humanity infuses all the others, even when we ignore it—and even when we elevate it and separate it from the others.

It has troubled me over the years to observe pastors who claim God's guidance in the midst of circumstances they ardently seek to disregard. An easy way for a pastor to play a spiritual trump card is to utter the words, "God has spoken to me." Too often, that kind of self-assurance is masking mounds of issues that need to be faced and dealt with. If you believe that you know God's will for a specific situation but have not honestly faced your own frailty in it, I question your discernment.

One way that church members become disheartened with faith is when pastors abuse their spiritual status. Speaking and acting on behalf of the gospel never should be taken lightly! When you leave your church, you want its members to thank God that you were with them, not breathe a sigh of relief or walk away, never to return. Understanding the intricacies of cultural capital is one way to help you maintain spiritual humility: As pastor, you are never in control as much as you think.

FAITH AS *TELOS*

As pastors, we regularly need to give our current ministries the longer view. We have to trust that God can use what we do in our congregations, even long past our tenure with them. We might not be satisfied with their response, especially if they are in the weakening phase. Yet, if we are "wise as serpents, and innocent as doves," we will have planted theological seeds that still have a chance to sprout and grow. Americans tend to be in a hurry; we want to see results now. In parish ministry, however, not everything that matters can be measured easily or occur quickly.

One motif in the Bible is that of "the next thing." The story of God's people in scripture does not end at one point in time or with one wonderful event or attainment. Instead, it continues to emerge, always in relationship to what has gone before. This tie between former things and new things is expressed dramatically in Isaiah 43:16–21 ("I am about to do a new thing") and Revelation 21:1–5 ("See, I am making all things new"). The *telos* of God, the fullness and completion of all things, eludes our fleeting efforts. It is in the hands of the Creator, who has called some of us to the fearful task of leading those whom God has brought together.

As pastors, may we understand that our calling is to orbit around getting along with our churches. May we see this challenge as a necessary step toward doing ministry that makes a difference for the gospel. May we be humble enough to put ourselves in God's hands amidst an imperfect community. May we appreciate the cultural relevance of being the spiritual and theological leader of these people. May we be patient enough to be genuinely surprised by what our partnership with them produces. Remember, it is never about us but about what they can do, because we have helped them to see the Way.

Appendix

For Denominational Officials

CUT OFF AT THE PASS

Y EARS AGO, I was searching for another pastoral call. All of my papers had been prepared and submitted properly, and I had made an initial contact with Rev. Jameson, the person in our regional denominational office who helped pastors and churches find each other. Rev. Jameson had met me on more than one occasion and now had a copy of my dossier. I began to find out which churches had openings; one of them was just what I was looking for. The community in which this church was located also was appealing and would not require much of a move, so I let Rev. Jameson know that I was interested in this particular position.

Weeks passed as I continued to seek out other pastoral openings and send them my dossier. I had expected by that time to hear from that one church that I had mentioned to Rev. Jameson. Finally, I called him to find out what he knew. Over the telephone, he told me in so many words that they were looking for someone different from me.

I was stunned. How could Rev. Jameson know what they wanted and whether I "had it" or not? In the next few days, I came to comprehend the situation more fully. I realized that Rev. Jameson had told them that they probably would not be interested in me. My position at the time was in a small church in a small town, while the church in which I was interested was large and suburban. Even though I was seeking a staff position, for which I had ample experience, Rev. Jameson had concluded that I would not fit in. Because of my rural setting, I wore casual clothes and, at times, a full beard. The other church was in a growing, business-oriented suburb, where men usually wore suits and ties and were clean shaven.

It took some time for me to get over feeling bitter that Rev. Jameson had undermined my chances for this potential call based on where I lived and how I dressed. In retrospect, however, I probably would not have enjoyed that position as much as I had thought. If this were going to be a church that judged a book by its cover, then perhaps it would not have been a good match. Yet, I would have preferred that Rev. Jameson had handled the situation differently. He could have put in a favorable word to the search committee for me, limiting his comments to my pastoral strengths. Then he could have suggested to me that, if I were asked for an interview, I should wear a suit and tie and think like a professional.

DILEMMAS IN MATCHING

If one of your denominational responsibilities is either to appoint pastors to churches or to recommend pastoral candidates to search committees, you often face the dilemmas to which I have alluded in this episode. You have multiple, sometimes conflicting, demands on your office. Yet it seems to me that paying attention to productive fits between pastors and churches can only enhance the overall potency of what your position requires of you. When the congregations under your care are strong, the greater the opportunity for strong gospel witness. Denominations directly benefit when their churches are strong and growing.[1]

This book has been designed to be used by pastors who are active in parish ministry. If you have read the preceding chapters, you know that my concern is to give pastors a practical, cultural frame of reference for navigating the intricacies and opportunities in their congregations. From your vantage point within your denomination's structure, you know that pastors face some pretty complex dynamics when they first walk into a new parish. As a model, "cultural capital" furnishes pastors with a set of tools that they can use to make their labors more fruitful.

This brief appendix assumes that you have read the chapters and are seeking to consider specifically how this material can aid you in furthering matches that will bless the pastor, the congregation, and the community at large. "Good matches" might not always look suitable on the surface. We need to dig deeper, to find out what both pastor and parish are looking for. Beyond this sometimes elusive information is the more significant question, "Can they grow with each other?" The following suggestions are organized first for all placement-related officers. These are followed by separate recommendations for officials who work with appointments and for calls.

GENERAL INSIGHTS

Perhaps the most basic point to note first is that, within your jurisdiction, culture is deep and varied. You know this already, even if you have not ever used technical terms to describe it. In your diocese, synod, conference, presbytery, or region, there are cultures shaped by class, orality, ethnic heritage, generation, and so on. Each one of the congregations in your region has its own idiosyncratic culture, reflecting various mixtures of these cultural streams. You experience these and many other cultural confluences (or lack thereof!) as you interact with all of these churches and their local settings. Simply trying to interpret beyond the artifacts to the shared assumptions can be overwhelming for someone in your position.

Your denomination and regional jurisdiction also has a culture and its own assumptions. Seek to become as aware as you can about these assumptions. Learn the meanings beyond the rituals and practices. Assess your relation to these assumptions; how deeply embedded are you in them? In the midst of your denominational culture, how much marginality have you managed to maintain? Insight and marginality strengthen your ability to serve well.

If your denomination is one of the old "mainline" traditions, there are a number of recently published resources that can give you valuable perspective. One of the most readable and applicable is *Rerouting the Protestant Mainstream*.[2] This succinct work discusses research on affiliation and participation patterns in American religion in a way that makes sense.[3] The authors, Kirk Hadaway and David Roozen, then apply the research findings in practical ways, both for congregations and for denominations.

Implications for structure, vision, leadership and worship also are presented. Hadaway and Roozen have produced a very revealing, useful book. It is the one book right now that, if I could do it, I would give to every mainline pastor and denominational official in North America. Even if your denomination is not part of this traditional religious "mainstream," you will find insights in this book that will help your churches.

Rerouting the Protestant Mainstream frames its discussion with applied sociology, yet the relevance for cultural interpretations becomes evident. For instance, paying attention to factors within the church's environment leads us to recognize the "soft" side of environment, its cultural complexities.[4] Hadaway and Roozen argue that declining denominations that want to grow again need to become more like movements and less like institutions.[5] The cultural dynamics in a religious movement are distinctly different from those of a well-established denomination.

My second basic point is a suggestion that, as a denominational official, you teach yourself to frame potential matches between pastors and churches in terms of culture. The purpose of this exercise is not to maintain a form of stasis within the congregation to which it has become comfortable. It is, rather, to find pastors who are willing and able to read and honor the culture that they find, as an integral part of their pastoral strategy. Culture theory helps us appreciate that no congregation can stand still. Pastors who help the church grow and change in the long run are those who attend also to what the church is like when they arrive.

Consider, for example, the concepts of life cycle. As you think about various congregations in your judicatory, can you detect the different church phases among them? Which ones are younger, still very fluid, and making their way? Which ones are established, relatively strong but less flexible? Which ones are showing the effects of life cycle weakening, whether they realize it or not? How do these differences in life cycle phases affect the leadership needs of each given congregation? It is sobering to think that many of our churches are declining and thus become distracted trying to "fix" their situation with a new technique or program. Pastors who are skilled at reading the culture of life cycle phases will approach a new position sensitively and creatively.

Culture theory can be helpful to you in other ways. Questions like the following can further stimulate your own creative activity as you engage the task of strengthening pastors with their parishes:

- How can you help candidates for ordination prepare to discern cultural dynamics?
- What resources does your committee of ordained ministry use to support pastors and churches?
- What continuing education events are available for pastors to attend that would provide a more organic analysis of congregations?

APPOINTMENT OFFICIALS

Since you have a great influence on the selection of pastors for particular parishes, let us examine more closely the matter of a cultural approach to matches. In deciding each year which pastors will serve where, you have a number of factors to consider, some of them more obvious and some of them delicate and private. Even though you have the authority to move pastors, you want to use it in a way that will foster trust in your office. What would the matching process be like if you include cultural capital in the mix? You would ask questions of analysis such as:

- How do the layers of culture (macro-, meso-, micro-) manifest themselves in distinct ways in each congregation?
- Which parishes are in which phases? which ones are open to self-insight?
- Which pastors know how to learn and adapt their style to the congregation?
- If a pastor is well suited for a certain charge, but the parish might think at first that she or he does not "fit," how do you persuade them that the appointment will benefit them?
- Which declining congregations are more likely to respond to a committed, sensitive pastor ready to help them turn things around?

In your responsibilities, you also find out about pastor-parish matches that are not working well. (It would be best if you found out about problems early, before they have escalated into a "win-lose" contest.) How would you utilize material from chapter 4 ("Effective Delivery") and chapter 6 ("Handling Conflict") to help both parties find constructive ways to continue? Is there a way to intervene in times of trouble without taking sides with either the pastor or the parish, but for the good of both?

Culture theory can help presiding elders, district superintendents, and others mediate potential problems with greater skill and confidence. As we saw earlier, cultural interpretation reduces the need to affix blame. It does so by reframing the situation in terms of artifacts, values, and assumptions. Cultural framing offers a way for everyone to understand more about why potential differences surface. Both the pastor and the parish can use such insight in later matches as well; they will have strengthened their respective cultural capital. I can imagine a team of persons within your judicatory who are trained to furnish these services.

Cultural capital also can help you in deciding pastoral moves. Chapter 7 covers many of the move issues from the standpoint of the pastor: These can be adapted by bishops and presiding elders. A cultural frame helps move beyond both demographic and anecdotal impressions of a congregation. A deeper comprehension of the congregation gives you a better feel for each church's vitality and adaptability. Your conversations with pastors or superintendents then focus on parish needs for the coming year and what the pastor will be bringing to lead the church. Determining how well the adoption process has developed will be a key element in anticipating a pastor's future effectiveness.

Using cultural capital as an interpretive and strategic resource in no way should be seen as creating a naive attitude toward pastor-parish relations. Rather, it can help those pastors under your charge to be more realistic. Both opportunities and hassles arise in any appointment. It makes a tremendous difference to the vitality of the parish if the pastor can keep himself or herself marginal enough to the parish to do effective ministry. You and your team can help pastors learn how to maintain such a healthy marginality.

CALL OFFICIALS

While you who are part of call traditions technically do not appoint pastors, your participation in search processes nonetheless can be instrumental. Many of the questions posed in the previous section can be easily adjusted for your role with pastoral searches. Some of them might read then as follows:

- How much does your word influence a search committee?
- How much cultural capital do you have with the particular congregation?
- How did you develop that capital; what might you have overlooked?
- What opportunities and needs do you see, in terms of culture and life cycle, in the searching churches? How do you discuss these with the search committee? With candidates?
- How is the culture of your judicatory symbolized in your churches? What do you expect of new pastors?
- What models do you currently use in discerning whether an open church and a candidate might be suitable for healthy ministry together?
- How do you help a pastor thinking about moving figure out what to do?

Since your authority normally does not extend to the actual decisions that pastors and churches make, you have to function more in terms of persuasion. Answering questions like those in this appendix aids you in being more astute in your contributions, more helpful to the match that is made in due course.

A WORD ABOUT GOD

Christian theology affirms that the Holy Spirit is present in the midst of the community of faith. Christian believers trust that the God who creates and redeems also empowers. Our faith includes trusting that the Holy Spirit is at work to bring God's aims for the world into actuality.

So God, then, is interested especially in the vitality of the many forms of Christian community. They themselves are vessels chosen for a distinct mission within God's larger scheme. Those who serve these vessels as pastors, therefore, play a unique role. God is concerned about who serves as pastors and who serves where.

Any Christian sage can tell you that our faith is not about magic. We do not seek to control God, as if our interests were all that mattered. Rather, we aim, even as congregations, to give ourselves to God's purposes in the larger scheme of things. To be Christian is to put ourselves in a position of dealing periodically with new things. Congregations need pastors who are sensitive in this way.

I know that you who help churches and pastors to find each other and live together pray for strength and wisdom. Sometimes, in certain moments, it is all that we can do. I hope that you seek the Spirit's guidance as you engage in this process. Then I hope that you will cast those decisions into the wind, trusting that the Spirit will be at work even in what you say and do. It is no less than what we hope our pastors and churches will do as well.

Notes

PREFACE

1. As an example, an anecdotal account of some of the dynamics of American Chinese cross-cultural encounters, with a concern for multicultural ministry, is part of Eric Law's concise but excellent book, *The Wolf Shall Dwell with the Lamb: A Spirituality for Leadership in a Multicultural Community* (St. Louis, Mo.: Chalice Press, 1993). Law's primary thesis is that, even in churches trying to be racially and ethnically inclusive, there tend to be power imbalances based in cultural differences.

Interest in congregational culture was stimulated by James Hopewell's *Congregation: Stories and Structures*, ed. Barbara G. Wheeler (Philadelphia: Fortress Press, 1987). Since its publication, the discipline of "congregational studies" has emerged. Its focus tends to be sociological and research-based; see esp. *Studying Congregations*, ed. Nancy Ammerman et al. (Nashville, Tenn.: Abingdon Press, 1998).

The effects of culture on congregations are also illustrated in Massey and McKinney's summary of the development of the African American church; they discuss the influence of the African village and chieftain, the role of emotion, transitions in pastoral roles from rural to urban settings, etc. See Floyd Massey Jr. and Samuel Berry McKinney, *Church Administration in the Black Perspective* (Valley Forge, Penn.: Judson Press, 1976), chaps. 1 and 2.

2. A brief, general discussion of culture in a church context may be found in my book, *Futuring Your Church: Finding Your Vision and Making It Work* (Cleveland: United Church Press, 1999), 16–19, and in Lovett H. Weems Jr., *Church Leadership: Vision, Team, Culture, and Integrity* (Nashville, Tenn.: Abingdon Press, 1993), chap. 4.

3. Massey and McKinney, *Church Administration in the Black Perspective*, 56–57.

4. The French scholar Pierre Bourdieu utilized the concept of cultural capital (along with the notion of "linguistic capital") in interpreting research on what he called "cultural reproduction"; see Pierre Bourdieu and Jean-Claude Passeron, *Reproduction in Education, Society, and Culture*, book 2, trans. Richard Nice (London: SAGE Publications, 1977), chap. 1, "Cultural Capital and Pedagogic Communication," esp. 73–76 and 82–83. Bourdieu has been extensively applied by other scholars to interpret research in art, history, architecture, education, sociology, and so on.

5. Anthony J. Gittins, *Gifts and Strangers: Meeting the Challenge of Inculturation* (New York: Paulist Press, 1989).

6. Ibid., xi–xii.

7. See, for instance, Anthony Giddens, *Modernity and Self-identity: Self and Society in the Late Modern Age* (Palo Alto, Calif.: Stanford University Press, 1991) and Richard H. Brown, *A Poetic for Sociology: Toward a Logic of Discovery for the Human Sciences* (Cambridge University Press, 1977).

CHAPTER 1

1. The following explanation of the three levels of culture is drawn from Edgar H. Schein's *Organizational Culture and Leadership*, 2d ed. (San Francisco: Jossey-Bass Publishers, 1992), chap. 2.

2. For an enumeration of the tasks of "internal integration," see ibid., chap. 5.

3. For an enumeration of the organization's tasks in adapting to its surroundings, see ibid., chap. 4.

4. As suggested in ibid., 20–22.

5. Ibid., 94, 124, for references to the relationship between an organization's "host culture" and its developing shared assumptions.

6. Most of the concepts in this section I have articulated myself. A brief summary of them can be found in my book, *Futuring Your Church: Finding Your Vision and Making It Work* (Cleveland: United Church Press, 1999), 41–42.

7. In his discussion of human nature as a dimension of culture from which shared assumptions are drawn, Schein refers to the "host culture" of an organization. The context for Schein's comment is cross-cultural and highlights the general point made here about hosts; see *Organizational Culture and Leadership*, 124.

8. Anthony J. Gittins, *Gifts and Strangers: Meeting the Challenge of Inculturation* (New York: Paulist Press, 1989).

9. Tex Sample, *Ministry in an Oral Culture: Living with Will Rogers, Uncle Remus, and Minnie Pearl* (Louisville, Ky.: Westminster/John Knox Press, 1994).

10. Ibid., chaps. 1 and 2.

11. Ibid., 6.

12. Statements in this paragraph refer to the work of William Strauss and Neil Howe, *Generations: The History of America's Future, 1584 to 2069* (New York: William Morrow, 1991), esp. chap. 1.

13. For a quick summary of characteristics of the four generations in the cycle, see ibid., 74.

14. A summary of this research and its implications is found in C. Kirk Hadaway and David A. Roozen, *Rerouting the Protestant Mainstream: Sources of Growth and Opportunities for Change* (Nashville, Tenn.: Abingdon Press, 1995), in the second chap., "Making the Church Choice," esp. 40–42.

CHAPTER 2

1. Anthony J. Gittins, *Gifts and Strangers: Meeting the Challenge of Inculturation* (New York: Paulist Press, 1989), chap. 5.

2. Ibid., 115–24.

3. Ibid., 117.

4. Ibid., 121.

5. Ibid., 124–26.

6. Ibid.; Gittins cites, as he draws in several places on, the famous work of Arnold van Gennep, *The Rites of Passage* (London: Routledge, Kegan Paul, 1960/1977).

7. Gittins, *Gifts and Strangers*, 125–26.

8. The notion of "subculture" refers to a culture within the organization that not only shares some of the history, practices, and assumptions of the organization but also has developed its own particular emphasis. A "dominant subculture" is one that has more influence on the overall life of the organization than any of the other subcultures. These two concepts will be introduced later in this chapter and utilized later as well.

9. See Tex Sample, *Ministry in an Oral Culture: Living with Will Rogers, Uncle Remus, and Minnie Pearl* (Louisville, Ky.: Westminster/John Knox Press, 1994), 61, for his brief critique of Enlightenment attitudes towards traditional communities; note also statements such as the following: "The problem for most of us career professionals is that we have become so individualistic, so rational, and so efficiency-oriented that we fail to see that other people operate on a completely different basis," 66.

10. See ibid., chaps. 1 and 2.

11. Gittins, *Gifts and Strangers*, 121.

12. The process of an organization's founder taking the lead in creating its culture is described in some detail in Edgar H. Schein's *Organizational Culture and Leadership*, 2d ed. (San Francisco: Jossey-Bass Publishers, 1992), chaps. 11 and 12.

13. Schein discusses this strategy, in terms of general organizational management; see ibid., for example, 258, 315–16, and 371.

14. Ibid., 380.

CHAPTER 3

1. An easy-to-follow version of this contrast is found in Anthony G. Pappas's very readable piece, *Entering the World of the Small Church: A Guide for Leaders* (Washington, D.C.: Alban Institute, 1988), 10–13. Pappas's main point is anthropological, as is the framework of this book. That is, Pappas argues that small churches—by which he means typical congregations in a rural or small-town setting—function in a cultural setting that is not dictated by the values and practices of modern, industrial, urban-shaped society. In this regard, Pappas is making the same case as is Tex Sample, in the work cited earlier, *Ministry in an Oral Culture: Living with Will Rogers, Uncle Remus, and Minnie Pearl* (Louisville, Ky.: Westminster/John Knox Press, 1994), (though Sample adds working-class peoples in urban areas, too). Their distinction is significant, considering the likelihood that many pastors, throughout their vocational years, will serve heavily oral congregations at one time or another.

2. Lovett Weems refers to Tom Peters's phrase "Management by Wandering Around" in encouraging effective pastoral leaders to do "ministry by wandering around." See Lovett H. Weems Jr., *Church Leadership: Vision, Team, Culture and Integrity* (Nashville, Tenn.: Abingdon Press, 1993), 53. This notion can be adapted for small-town contexts as "ministry by hanging around."

3. Floyd Massey Jr. and Samuel Berry McKinney, *Church Administration in the Black Perspective* (Valley Forge, Penn.: Judson Press, 1976), 16–23.

4. Perhaps the best summary of this discussion, as adapted for a church context, is found in Weems, *Church Leadership*, chap. 2.

5. My book, *Futuring Your Church: Finding Your Vision and Making It Work* (Cleveland: United Church Press, 1999), is designed to help a congregation discern a fresh vision, one that will inspire and motivate congregations. It also is based on a cultural model and includes suggestions on how to put the espoused values stated in the vision (referred to in the book as the "stars of the constellation") to work in programming, administration, and developing constituencies (see chap. 6).

6. The ideas for the following discussion, and its relation to vision, derive from Ichak Adizes, *Corporate Lifecycles: How and Why Corporations Grow and Die and What to Do about It* (Englewood Cliffs, N. J.: Prentice Hall, 1988), 117–33, 141–47. See also my arrangement of this material in *Futuring Your Church*, chap. 6.

CHAPTER 4

1. Information in this section is based on Edgar H. Schein's *Organizational Culture and Leadership*, 2d ed. (San Francisco: Jossey-Bass Publishers, 1992), chaps. 11 and 12.

2. See ibid., chap. 16, for a description of this organizational phase and the challenges that it brings to leadership.

3. For insight into organizational theory that helps to shape the comments in this section, see Ichak Adizes, *Corporate Lifecycles: How and Why Corporations Grow and Die and What to Do about It* (Englewood Cliffs, N. J.: Prentice Hall, 1988), chaps. 3 and 10.

CHAPTER 5

1. This phrase is similar to the one suggested by Lovett H. Weems Jr. in his book, *Church Leadership: Vision, Team, Culture and Integrity* (Nashville, Tenn.: Abingdon Press, 1993), "[a vision is] a picture of a preferred future (39)."

2. The ideas in this section are summarized by James Luther Adams in his essay, "The Voluntary Principle," published in a collection of his writings, *Voluntary Associations: Socio-cultural Analyses and Theological Interpretation*, ed. J. Ronald Engel (Chicago: Exploration Press, 1986), 175–78.

3. Ibid., 252.

4. The phenomenon of American church choice has been well documented over the last generation, as we noted in chap. 1. See C. Kirk Hadaway and David A. Roozen, *Rerouting the Protestant Mainstream: Sources of Growth and Opportunities for Change* (Nashville:, Tenn. Abingdon Press, 1995), chap. 2.

5. Weems, *Church Leadership*, 25.

6. For an elaboration of the components of vision and how a church can discern fresh vision, see my book, *Futuring Your Church: Finding Your Vision and Making It Work* (Cleveland: United Church Press, 1999), chaps. 2–5.

7. For an excellent summary of the issues of organizational culture, learning, and leadership, see Edgar H. Schein's *Organizational Culture and Leadership*, 2d ed. (San Francisco: Jossey-Bass Publishers, 1992), chaps. 18 and 19.

8. See ibid., 298–303, for a summary of the organizational change process and the importance of anticipating emotional reactions by members.

9. See Ichak Adizes, *Corporate Lifecycles: How and Why Corporations Grow and Die and What to Do about It* (Englewood Cliffs, N. J.: Prentice Hall, 1988), 162.

10. As per Schein, *Organizational Culture and Leadership*, 363.

11. The following six qualities are summarized and adapted from ibid., 386–91.

12. See, for instance, Norman Shawchuck and Gustave Rath, *Benchmarks of Quality in the Church: 21 Ways to Continuously Improve the Content of Your Ministry* (Nashville, Tenn.: Abingdon Press, 1994), chap. 2; David Young, *A New Heart and a New Spirit: A Plan for Renewing Your Church* (Valley Forge, Penn.: Judson Press, 1994), chap. 6; William M. Easum, *Sacred Cows Make Gourmet Burgers: Ministry Anytime, Anywhere, by Anybody* (Nashville, Tenn.: Abingdon Press, 1995); and John Ed Mathison, *Tried and True: Eleven Principles of Church Growth from Frazer Memorial United Methodist Church* (Nashville, Tenn.: Discipleship Resources, 1992), chap. 8.

13. For the main points in this section, see Schein, *Organizational Culture and Leadership*, 382–83 and 312.

14. Weems, *Church Leadership*, 34–35.

15. Again, see Schein, *Organizational Culture and Leadership*, esp. chaps. 15 and 16.

16. For more information, see my book, *Futuring Your Church*, chap. 6.

17. Adizes refers to the "who" function (which he calls "Integrate/Include") as "organic"; see Adizes, *Corporate Lifecycles*, 123–33.

18. For a clear, useful explanation of vision, see again Weems, *Church Leadership*, chap. 2.

19. Adizes' insight here is instructive: "I do not use the word *adapt* to changing environment. . . . Adapting means being reactive, not proactive. We must proact, project what the future is going to be, and then do something about it. We don't have the luxury of waiting for the future so we decide then what to do," *Corporate Lifestyles*, 123. This comment, written in the context of the business world, is just as relevant for churches.

CHAPTER 6

1. Carl S. Dudley and Earle Hilgert, *New Testament Tensions and the Contemporary Church* (Philadelphia: Fortress Press, 1987).

2. Ibid., chap. 1.

3. Ibid., chap. 2.

4. Ibid., chap 3.

5. Ibid., 134.

6. Ibid., 129–30.

7. The literature treating pastor-church conflict is extensive enough that it cannot be summarized here in any comprehensive way. References in pastoral books to conflict began to appear by the 1960s; see, e.g., James D. Glasse, *Profession: Minister: Confronting the Identity Crisis of the Parish Clergy* (Nashville, Tenn.: Abingdon Press, 1968), 13, and Glasse's subsequent *Putting*

It Together in the Parish (Nashville, Tenn.: Abingdon Press, 1972), chap. 9, "Learning to Fight Like Christians in the Church." Donald P. Smith's *Clergy in the Cross-Fire: Coping with Role Conflicts in the Ministry* (Philadelphia: Westminster Press, 1973), combined research findings with sociological theory and organizational practice to assist pastors. Speed Leas of the Alban Institute gained a nationwide reputation for developing widely used conflict management tools for churches; see Speed Leas and Paul Kittlaus, *Church Fights* (Philadelphia: Westminster Press, 1973); see also Leas, *Leadership and Conflict* (Nashville, Tenn.: Abingdon Press, 1982). Leas also has published resources with The Alban Institute, Bethesda, Maryland. We already have seen above Dudley and Hilgert's contribution through New Testament studies. Hugh F. Halverstadt drew heavily on organizational theory to create an ethically based process for churches in conflict; see his *Managing Church Conflict* (Louisville, Ky.: Westminster/John Knox Press, 1991). Many other titles, of varying depth and applicability, have appeared since about 1985, around the time that new literature on church growth began to crest. See any connection?

8. From R. Robert Cueni, *What Ministers Can't Learn in Seminary* (Nashville, Tenn.: Abingdon Press, 1988), 83–84, as told in Lovett Weems, *Church Leadership: Vision, Team, Culture and Integrity* (Nashville: Abingdon Press, 1993), 100–01.

9. For a summary of oral culture, see again Tex Sample, *Ministry in an Oral Culture: Living with Will Rogers, Uncle Remus, and Minnie Pearl* (Louisville, Ky.: Westminster/John Knox Press, 1994), esp. chaps. 1 and 2; for notes on the hospitality of hosts to strangers, see again Anthony J. Gittins, *Gifts and Strangers: Meeting the Challenge of Inculturation* (New York: Paulist Press, 1989), 115–19.

10. Sample critiques the culture that gives rise to seminary-trained pastors: "Professional and literate people . . . are usually more mobile geographically, less local in orientation, and not usually involved in extended communal relations. They tend to be more individualistic . . . more goal-oriented . . . more utilitarian . . . more linear in focus . . . and less 'complicated' by 'lateral' and multidimensional communal concerns," *Ministry in an Oral Culture*, 54–55.

11. For a summary of this model, which in the West dominated the twentieth century, see Charles Perrow, *Complex Organizations: A Critical Essay*, 3rd ed. (New York: McGraw-Hill, 1986), chap. 1, esp. 3–6; see also Joseph McCann, *Church and Organization: A Sociological and Theological Inquiry* (London: Associated University Presses, 1993), chap. 2, esp. 35–37.

12. A concise but very fine discussion of pastoral integrity can be found in Weems's *Church Leadership*, chap. 5, "Integrity." There Weems argues, for instance, that personal integrity is not grounded in following some kind of legalistic standards: "Integrity has far more to do with consistency between articulated values and behavior than it does with adherence to some prescribed code," 123.

13. Floyd Massey Jr. and Samuel Berry McKinney, *Church Administration in the Black Perspective* (Valley Forge, Penn.: Judson Press, 1976), 11.

14. See Edgar H. Schein, *Organizational Culture and Leadership*, 2d ed. (San Francisco: Jossey-Bass Publishers, 1992), chap. 11, as well as chap. 12, "How Founders and Leaders Embed and Transmit Culture."

15. See Schein's definition of culture: "A pattern of shared basic assumptions that the group learned as it solved its problems . . . that has worked well enough to be considered valid. . . . ," ibid., 12.

16. These characteristics are adapted from ibid., 254–58.

17. See Schein's comments about organizational leaders and marginality, ibid., 380, 383, and 386.

CHAPTER 7

1. In the African American Baptist tradition, for instance, long pastorates are not uncommon; see the brief explanation of reasons why, and a summary of research, in Floyd Massey Jr. and Samuel Berry McKinney, *Church Administration in the Black Perspective* (Valley Forge, Penn.: Judson Press, 1976), 25–28.

2. These phases were outlined in this book in chap. 6, under the subsection "Assumptions and the Life Cycle."

3. An apt illustration of this point is found in Tex Sample's *Ministry in an Oral Culture: Living with Will Rogers, Uncle Remus, and Minnie Pearl* (Louisville, Ky.: Westminster/John Knox Press, 1994), 45–46, in which Sample supervised a student pastor in a management by objective (MBO) project, at the student's request and over Sample's objections. After the student graduated, he was appointed to another charge and the church dropped the MBO process. They had agreed to do it because they cared about their student pastor and were willing to help him work on something in which he was interested, even though they knew that they would not use the process again.

4. For an incisive analysis of the problems facing an organization and its founder in the younger life cycle phase, see Ichak Adizes, *Corporate Lifecycles: How and Why Corporations Grow and Die and What to Do about It* (Englewood Cliffs, N. J.: Prentice Hall, 1988), 34–55. His comment on page 47 is instructive: "A founder with a Lone Ranger style of management . . . needs to change his [sic] style."

5. For a discussion of an organic view of nature and humanity, with implications for Christian theology and congregations, see Bernard Lee's *The Becoming of the Church: A Process Theology of the Structure of Christian Experience* (New York: Paulist Press, 1974).

APPENDIX

1. For a sociological analysis of these relationships, especially congregation to denomination, see David A. Roozen, "Denominations Grow as Individuals Join Congregations," *Church and Denominational Growth: What Does (and Does Not) Cause Growth or Decline,* ed. David A. Roozen and C. Kirk Hadaway (Nashville, Tenn.: Abingdon Press, 1993), 15–35; see also the introduction to part 1, "Denominational Growth and Decline," by Hadaway and Roozen, 37–45.

2. Hadaway and Roozen, *Rerouting the Protestant Mainstream: Sources of Growth and Opportunities for Change* (Nashville: Abingdon Press, 1995).

3. Ibid., chap. 1, "Where We Are, and from Whence We Came," and chap. 2, "Making the Church Choice."

4. Ibid., e.g., 63–64; 126–27; see also the discussion of the dramatic change in American culture, away from a "cultural center," 111–12.

5. Ibid., 91–95.

Other Books from The Pilgrim Press

FUTURING YOUR CHURCH
Finding Your Vision and Making It Work
GEORGE B. THOMPSON JR.

In *Futuring Your Church*, church leaders explore a congregation's heritage, its current context, and its theological bearings. From the insights gleaned, members can discern what God is currently calling the church to do in this time and place. Once the vision is found, the book then provides a simple organizational model for applying the vision and for making it work.

0-8298-1331-4/paper/128 pages/$14.95

THE BIG SMALL CHURCH BOOK
DAVID R. RAY

Over sixty percent of churches have fewer than seventy-five people in attendance on Sunday. This book contains information on everything from practical business matters to spiritual development. Big churches can learn much here as well.

0-8298-0936-8/paper/256 pages/$15.95

WONDERFUL WORSHIP IN SMALLER CHURCHES
DAVID R. RAY

A valuable follow-up to the popular *The Big Small Church Book*, this resource is specifically designed for pastors and lay leaders who are responsible for leading worship in small churches. Ray provides sample services, sermons, guidelines for worship leaders, and a model survey for evaluating worship.

0-8298-1400-0/paper/192 pages/$19.95

THE HEALING CHURCH

Practical Programs for Health Ministries

ABIGAIL RIAN EVANS

Evans demonstrates what is not needed to invent health ministries, but to recapture the spirit of the church as a health institution, both spiritual and physical. She further shows what practical programs exist in the world today and why these programs are important for the church to embrace and develop.

0-8298-1340-3/paper/288 pages/$23.95

BECOMING A NEW CHURCH

Reflections on Faith and Calling

MALCOLM WARFORD

Since church membership has entered into a period of rapid decline, the church is being challenged to renew and redefine itself and its ministries by liberating itself from past constraints and crafting new ways of being "the church." Warford invites his readers to think of themselves as pilgrims in a community where there are no clearly marked road signs, but where we have a shared memory of Jesus who made us free to live open to the world and its potential for transformation.

0-8298-1387-x/paper/128 pages/$14.95

THE POLITICS OF WORSHIP

Reforming the Language and Symbols of Liturgy

WILLIAM JOHNSON EVERETT

Everett closely examines the political theology of worship and proposes a ritual practice that strives to be consistent with a Christian ethic of inclusiveness and mutuality. It is this practice that will help move Christian worship beyond the old language and symbols and into a new, truly inclusive paradigm.

0-8298-1341-1/paper/160 pages/$17.95

To order these or any other books from The Pilgrim Press call or write to:

The Pilgrim Press
700 Prospect Ave E
Cleveland OH 44115-1100

PHONE ORDERS: 800.537.3394
FAX ORDERS: 216.736.2206

Or order from our Web site at <www.pilgrimpress.com>.

Please include shipping charges of $4.00 for the first book and 75¢ for each additional book.

Prices subject to change without notice.